Praise for Aaron Shepard's *Stories on Stage*

— SECOND EDITION —

What? Don't have time to write up your own scripts for reader's theater? Not to worry. Aar̶̶̶̶ ̶̶̶̶ ̶̶̶̶ th his stellar scripts— perfect for duplic̶ ̶ ̶ s, and bringing to life. This is one must-̶ ̶ ̶

Still For

One of the challenges of teaching is instilling in our students a love for reading. By transforming imaginative stories by some of our favorite authors into clever scripts, Aaron Shepard once again provides the means for teachers to nurture a passion for the written word. This second edition of *Stories On Stage* is a most worthwhile addition to your cache of reading strategies that work.

> **Susan Finney**
> **Author,** *Keep the Rest of the Class Reading and Writing While You Teach Small Groups*

— FIRST EDITION —

Reader's theater gets a boost from this collection. . . . The scripts are simple and direct, multicultural, and easily reproducible for classroom use.

> **Ilene Cooper**
> *Booklist* **(American Library Association), Jan. 1, 1994**

An intriguing, well-rounded collection. . . . The tone and content of source material is effectively preserved.

> *The Horn Book Guide,* **July-Dec. 1993**

Give kids a script and watch them act. . . . Shepard's talent as a storyteller shines out in his adaptations.

> **Jan Lieberman**
> *TNT: Tips & Titles of Books,* **Fall 1993**

A well-written collection. . . . These scripts will inspire young actors to read the books.

> **Penny Peck**
> *Bayviews* **(Assoc. of Children's Librarians), Nov. 1993**

Also by Aaron Shepard

Professional Resources

Readers on Stage: Resources for Reader's Theater
Folktales on Stage: Scripts for Reader's Theater
The Business of Writing for Children
Folktales to Tell (forthcoming)

Picture Books and Easy Readers

The Adventures of Mouse Deer: Tales of Indonesia and Malaysia
The Legend of Lightning Larry
King o' the Cats
The Princess Mouse: A Tale of Finland
Master Man: A Tall Tale of Nigeria
Lady White Snake: A Tale From Chinese Opera
The Sea King's Daughter: A Russian Legend
The Baker's Dozen: A Saint Nicholas Tale
The Magic Brocade: A Tale of China
Forty Fortunes: A Tale of Iran
The Crystal Heart: A Vietnamese Legend
Master Maid: A Tale of Norway
The Maiden of Northland: A Hero Tale of Finland
The Gifts of Wali Dad: A Tale of India and Pakistan
The Enchanted Storks: A Tale of Bagdad
The Legend of Slappy Hooper: An American Tall Tale
Savitri: A Tale of Ancient India
Two-Eyes (forthcoming)

Chapter Books and Novels

Monkey: A Superhero Tale of China
Timothy Tolliver and the Bully Basher
Rhiannon: A Celtic Legend (forthcoming)

Stories

ON STAGE

**Children's Plays for Reader's Theater
(or Readers Theatre), With 15 Play Scripts
From 15 Authors**

Aaron Shepard

— SECOND EDITION —

Shepard Publications
Olympia, Washington

ISBN-13: 978-0-938497-22-6
ISBN-10: 0-938497-22-7

Library of Congress Control Number: 2005903075
Library of Congress subject headings:
Readers' theater
Children's plays

The first edition of *Stories on Stage* was published by The H. W. Wilson
Company, New York, 1993. This second edition retains most of the original
scripts, with improved formatting and expanded introductory info for each.

1.0

For Jean Wagner and the Chamber Readers

Contents—Short

Contents—Long

About This Book

Stories on Stage is a collection of reader's theater scripts for young readers, adapted from stories by fifteen different authors, including such popular ones as Louis Sachar, Nancy Farmer, and Roald Dahl. Each story was selected for its dramatic quality, literary value, and appeal to young people. Genres include fantasy, multicultural folktales, and humor.

The scripts may be freely copied, shared, and performed for any noncommercial purpose, except they may not be posted online without permission. Feel free to edit the scripts to serve the needs of your own readers.

A wide range of reading levels is included, with a focus on ages 8 to 15. Recommended reading age more or less progresses through the book, from younger to older.

A primary aim of reader's theater is to promote reading. To further this, it's good to have on hand one or more copies of the book or magazine story that the script is based on.

Above all, have fun with the scripts. Let your readers discover that reading is a treat.

About the Scripts

In the "long" table of contents, and at the beginning of each script, you'll find notation on genre, culture of origin or setting, theme, number of readers, suggested reader ages, and approximate reading time, as well as a brief description of the story.

Also at the beginning of each script is a list of roles. A reader, of course, can be assigned more than one role, as long as only one role is "onstage" at a time. When a script is short on female characters, it's common to cast females in male roles.

Roles listed in parentheses are unscripted, with no assigned speech, and usually optional. These roles can be given to surplus readers if your directing style includes stage movement or if you choose to add speeches or sounds for these readers. In the reader count, unscripted roles are indicated by the phrase "or more."

These scripts are designed to be photocopied for direct use by readers. (That's why all the page numbers in the scripts are at top right!) For performing, some kind of binder will be helpful.

About Staging

Of course, an actual stage is not required for reader's theater. *Stage* here refers simply to your performance area, which could be the front of a classroom, or an open space in a one-room library, or one end of a school gym or cafeteria. (Or a script could be used as a group reading exercise, with no performance area at all.)

It's best that you first read the script—or its source story—*to* the young people. Some scripts may be challenging, and effective modeling will lead to greater benefit and enjoyment.

The readers can underline or highlight their own parts in their copies of the script, marking only words to be spoken. (Yellow non-fluorescent marker works well.) Any unfamiliar words should be looked up and checked for pronunciation and meaning. Added stage directions can go in the script margins—preferably in pencil, to allow corrections.

Your readers might also prepare an introduction to the story, for use in performance. While an introduction should always mention the title and the author, it could also discuss source, author background, cultural background, theme, or context within a longer work. But it shouldn't give away the plot! Notes at the beginning of some scripts will provide starting points. Introductions are most effective when spoken informally, rather than read or memorized exactly.

With many of the scripts, you can produce a lively stereo effect by dividing your narrators between the two ends of your stage. For instance, with four narrators, place Narrators 1 and 2 at far left, and 3 and 4 at far right, as seen from the audience. To preserve this effect with fewer readers, assign the roles of Narrators 1 and 2 to one reader, and 3 and 4 to another.

In some scripts, particular narrators may relate mostly to particular characters. Notes at the start of those scripts will suggest positioning the characters near the corresponding narrators.

There are many styles of reader's theater. In the most traditional style:

- Readers are arranged in a row or a semicircle, standing up or sitting on high stools. Typically, narrators are placed at one or both ends, and major characters in the center.

- Scripts can be held in hand or set on music stands.

- Readers look straight out toward the audience or at an angle, rather than at each other.

- Characters "exit" by turning their backs to the audience. (Narrators don't normally exit.)
- "Scene changes"—jumps in time or place—can be shown by a group "freeze," followed by some kind of collective shift.

Chamber Readers, the group with which I trained and performed for five years, employs a style that is quite different, designed to appeal to young audiences. (For more details, see my book *Readers on Stage*.)

- Characters portray the action described in the story. Where possible, the portrayal is literal, with characters moving around the stage much as in a play. Where necessary, it's instead suggestive, as with simple mime devices like walking in place.
- Though narrators look mostly at the audience, characters look mostly at each other.
- Scripts in sturdy binders are held in one hand, leaving the other hand free for acting.
- A set of low stools and perhaps one or more high stools serve as versatile stage scenery or props.
- "Exits" and "scene changes" are handled much as in traditional reader's theater.

These scripts should lend themselves to either approach, or to any other you might choose. Feel free to create your own! There *are* rules in reader's theater, but luckily there is no one to enforce them.

About the Web Site

For more resources, please visit my Web site at www.aaronshep.com. From there, click on Aaron's RT Page (www.aaronshep.com/rt) to find many more scripts, plus other help with reader's theater.

To help you find what you need, the site includes a comprehensive search function, as well as indexes of all my stories and scripts—online and off—by title, genre, age, theme, country or region, historical period, ethnic group, religion, mythology, holiday, and activity.

And while you're visiting, be sure to sign up for my email bulletin to receive notice of new scripts and collections. There's always more to come!

Millions of Cats

By Wanda Gag

Adapted for reader's theater by Aaron Shepard, from Wanda Gag's picture book published by Coward-McCann, New York, 1928, and reprinted by Putnam & Grosset, New York, 1988

For more reader's theater, visit Aaron Shepard's RT Page at
www.aaronshep.com/rt

PREVIEW: An old man has trouble making a choice when he finds a hill quite covered with cats.

GENRE: Fantasy | READERS: 9 or more
CULTURE: —— | READER AGES: 7–11
THEME: Moderation; pride vs. humility | LENGTH: 6 minutes

ROLES: Narrators 1–4, Old Man, Old Woman, Kitty, Cats

NOTES: The classic *Millions of Cats* has been described as the first modern picture book. For best effect, place NARRATORS 1 and 2 at far left, and 3 and 4 at far right, as seen from the audience. At least two CATS are needed—but the more, the better! When they speak all at once, it should be randomly, not in unison, and can extend under other spoken parts as needed.

NARRATOR 1: Once upon a time, there was

OLD MAN: A very old man.

OLD WOMAN: And a very old woman.

NARRATOR 4: They lived in a nice clean house that had flowers all around it,

NARRATOR 2: except where the door was. But they couldn't be happy,

NARRATOR 3: because they were so very lonely.

OLD WOMAN: If we only had a cat!

NARRATOR 1: . . . sighed the very old woman.

OLD MAN: A cat?

NARRATOR 4: . . . asked the very old man.

OLD WOMAN: Yes, a sweet little fluffy cat.

NARRATOR 2: . . . said the very old woman.

OLD MAN: I will get you a cat, my dear.

NARRATOR 3: . . . said the very old man. And he set out to look for one.

NARRATOR 1: He climbed over the sunny hills.

NARRATOR 4: He trudged through the cool valleys.

NARRATOR 2: He walked a long, long time,

NARRATOR 3: and at last he came to a hill that was quite covered with cats.

CATS & KITTY: Mew, mew, mew . . . .

NARRATOR 1: Cats *here,*

NARRATOR 4: cats *there,*

NARRATORS 2 & 3: cats and kittens *everywhere.*

NARRATOR 1: *Hundreds* of cats,

NARRATOR 4: *thousands* of cats,

NARRATOR 2: *millions*

NARRATOR 2 & 3: and BILLIONS

NARRATORS 1, 2, 3, & 4: and *TRILLIONS* of cats.

OLD MAN: Oh! Now I can choose the prettiest cat and take it home with me!

NARRATOR 1: So he chose one. It was white. But just as he was about to leave,

NARRATOR 4: he saw another one, all black and white, and it seemed just as pretty as the first. So he took this one also. But then he saw

NARRATOR 2: a fuzzy gray kitten way over here that was every bit as pretty as the others. So he took it too. And now he saw,

NARRATOR 3: way down in a corner, one that he thought too lovely to leave. So he took this too. And just then,

NARRATOR 1: over here, the very old man found a kitten that was black and very beautiful.

OLD MAN: It would be a shame to leave *that* one.

NARRATOR 1: So he took it. And now, over there,

NARRATOR 4: he saw a cat that had brown and yellow stripes like a baby tiger.

OLD MAN: I simply must take it!

NARRATOR 4: And he did.

NARRATOR 2: And so it happened

NARRATOR 3: that every time the very old man looked up,

NARRATOR 1: he saw another cat that was so pretty,

NARRATOR 4: he could not bear to leave it.

NARRATOR 2: Before he knew it,

NARRATOR 3: he had chosen them all!

CATS & KITTY: Mew, mew, mew . . . .

NARRATOR 1: And so he went back over the sunny hills,

NARRATOR 4: and down through the cool valleys,

NARRATOR 2: to show all the pretty kittens

NARRATOR 3: to the very old woman.

NARRATOR 1: And all the hundreds of cats,

NARRATOR 4: thousands of cats,

NARRATOR 2: millions

NARRATOR 2 & 3: and billions

NARRATORS 1, 2, 3, & 4: and trillions of cats

NARRATOR 1: followed him.

CATS & KITTY: Mew, mew, mew . . . .

NARRATOR 1: They came to a pond.

CATS & KITTY: Mew, mew! We are thirsty!

NARRATOR 1: . . . cried the hundreds of cats,

NARRATOR 4: thousands of cats,

NARRATOR 2: millions

NARRATOR 2 & 3: and billions

NARRATORS 1, 2, 3, & 4: and trillions of cats.

OLD MAN: Well, here is a great deal of water.

NARRATOR 4: . . . said the very old man.

NARRATOR 2: Each cat took a sip of water.

CATS & KITTY: *(sip)*

NARRATOR 3: The pond was gone!

CATS & KITTY: Mew, mew! Now we are hungry!

NARRATOR 1: . . . cried the hundreds of cats,

NARRATOR 4: thousands of cats,

NARRATOR 2: millions

NARRATOR 2 & 3: and billions

NARRATORS 1, 2, 3, & 4: and trillions of cats.

OLD MAN: There is much grass on the hills.

NARRATOR 4: . . . said the very old man.

NARRATOR 2: Each cat ate a mouthful of grass.

CATS & KITTY: *(chew)*

NARRATOR 3: Not a blade was left!

CATS & KITTY: Mew, mew, mew . . . .

NARRATOR 1: Pretty soon, the very old woman saw them coming.

OLD WOMAN: My dear! What are you doing? I asked for one little cat, and what do I see?

> Cats here,
> Cats there,
> Cats and kittens everywhere!
> Hundreds of cats,
> Thousands of cats,
> Millions and billions and trillions of cats!

But we can never *feed* them all. They will eat us out of house and home!

OLD MAN: I never thought of that!

NARRATOR 4: . . . said the very old man.

OLD MAN: What shall we do?

NARRATOR 2: The very old woman thought for a while.

OLD WOMAN: *I* know! We will let the *cats* decide which one we should keep.

OLD MAN: Oh, yes!

NARRATOR 3: And the very old man called to the cats,

OLD MAN: Which one of you is the prettiest?

CATS: *I* am! . . . No, *I* am! . . . No, *I* am the prettiest! . . .

NARRATOR 1: . . . cried the hundreds of cats,

NARRATOR 4: thousands of cats,

NARRATOR 2: millions

NARRATOR 2 & 3: and billions

NARRATORS 1, 2, 3, & 4: and trillions of cats,

NARRATOR 1: for each cat thought *it* was the prettiest.

CATS: *I* am! . . . No, *I* am! . . . No, *I* am the prettiest! . . .

NARRATOR 1: And they began to quarrel. They bit

NARRATOR 4: and scratched

NARRATOR 2: and clawed each other

NARRATOR 3: and made such a great noise

NARRATOR 1: that the very old man

NARRATOR 4: and the very old woman

NARRATOR 2: ran into the house

NARRATOR 3: as fast as they could.

CATS: *I* am! . . . No, *I* am! . . . No, *I* am the prettiest! . . .

NARRATOR 1: But after a while the noise stopped. The very old man

NARRATOR 4: and the very old woman

NARRATOR 2: peeped out to see what had happened.

NARRATOR 3: They could not see a single cat!

OLD WOMAN: I think they must have eaten each other all up. It's too bad!

OLD MAN: But look!

NARRATOR 1: The very old man pointed to a bunch of high grass.

NARRATOR 4: In it sat one little frightened kitten.

NARRATOR 2: They went out and picked it up.

NARRATOR 3: It was thin and scraggly.

OLD WOMAN: Poor little kitty.

OLD MAN: *Dear* little kitty, how does it happen that you were not eaten up with all those hundreds and thousands and millions and billions and trillions of cats?

KITTY: Oh, I'm just a very homely little cat. So when you asked who was the prettiest, I didn't say anything. So nobody bothered about me.

NARRATOR 1: They took the kitten into the house.

NARRATOR 4: The very old woman gave it a warm bath and brushed its fur till it was soft and shiny.

NARRATOR 2: Every day, they gave it plenty of milk,

NARRATOR 3: and soon it grew nice and plump.

OLD WOMAN: And it is a very pretty cat, after all!

OLD MAN: It is the most beautiful cat in the whole world! I ought to know, for I've seen

Hundreds of cats,
Thousands of cats,
Millions and billions and trillions of cats!

And not *one* was as pretty as *this*.

Harriet

By Florence Parry Heide

Adapted for reader's theater by Aaron Shepard, from Florence Parry Heide's story in her book *Tales for the Perfect Child,* Lothrop, Lee & Shepard, New York, 1985

PREVIEW: Harriet was a very good whiner.

GENRE: Humor   READERS: 6
CULTURE: American   READER AGES: 7–11
THEME: Whining   LENGTH: 3 minutes

ROLES: Narrators 1–4, Harriet, Mother

NOTES: For best effect, place NARRATORS 1 and 2 at far left, and 3 and 4 at far right, as seen from the audience.

NARRATOR 1: Harriet was a very good whiner. She practiced and practiced, and so of course she got better and better at it.

NARRATOR 4: Practice makes perfect.

NARRATOR 2: Some children hardly *ever* whine. Can you believe that?

NARRATOR 3: So of course, they never get to be very *good* at it.

HARRIET: Can I have a piece of that blueberry pie?

NARRATOR 1: . . . Harriet asked her mother while her mother was fixing dinner.

NARRATOR 4: Guests were coming, and her mother wanted everything to be very nice.

MOTHER: No, Harriet. The pie is for after dinner. We're having roast beef.

NARRATOR 2: Children like Harriet are not interested in roast beef when they are interested in pie.

NARRATOR 3: Harriet used her best whiny voice.

HARRIET: I want a piece of *pie.*

MOTHER: I said no, and I mean no.

NARRATOR 1: Harriet's mother always liked to say what she meant.

NARRATOR 4: She started to make some nice tomato aspic.

HARRIET: Can I have some *pie,* can I have some *pie?*

MOTHER: Harriet, I told you, when I say no, I mean no!

HARRIET: But I want some *pie.*

MOTHER: Harriet—

HARRIET: Can I have some *pie?*

NARRATOR 2: Harriet's mother tried to concentrate on the aspic—

HARRIET: *Please* can I have some *pie?*

NARRATOR 2: but that was very hard to do, because Harriet was whining.

HARRIET: Why won't you give me some *pie? Why? Why? (whimpers)*

NARRATOR 3: Good whiners make it very hard for anyone to think of anything else.

MOTHER: Why don't you color in your nice new coloring book?

HARRIET: I want some pie *now.*

MOTHER: Dinner will be ready pretty soon.

HARRIET: But *I* want some pie NOW.

NARRATOR 1: A good whiner sticks to one subject.

HARRIET: *I want some pie.*

NARRATOR 4: A good whiner never gives up.

HARRIET: PLEASE can I have some *pie?*

NARRATOR 2: Harriet kept whining—

HARRIET: I want some *pie.* I want some *pie.* I want some *pie.*

NARRATOR 2: and her mother kept trying to get dinner ready.

HARRIET: *I . . . want . . . some . . .* PIE.

NARRATOR 3: Her mother burned the gravy.

MOTHER: *(shouting)* All right, all right! Have some PIE!

NARRATOR 1: She was very tired of hearing Harriet whine.

NARRATOR 4: Harriet stopped whining while she had her piece of pie.

NARRATOR 2: She always rested up between whines.

NARRATOR 3: That's what good whiners always do.

The Legend of Lightning Larry

By Aaron Shepard

Adapted for reader's theater by the author, from his picture book published by Scribners, New York, 1993

> For more reader's theater, visit Aaron Shepard's RT Page at
> **www.aaronshep.com/rt**

PREVIEW: A cowboy with a huge smile, a gun that shoots bolts of light, and a hankering for lemonade takes on Evil-Eye McNeevil's outlaw gang.

GENRE: Fables (original), tall tales, humor
CULTURE: American (Western frontier)
THEME: Peacemaking

READERS: 22 or more
READER AGES: 7–12
LENGTH: 8 minutes

ROLES: Citizens 1–8, Lightning Larry, Crooked Curt, Evil-Eye McNeevil, Dismal Dan, Devilish Dick, Dreadful Dave, Stinky Steve, Sickening Sid, Raunchy Ralph, Grimy Greg, Creepy Cal, Moldy Mike, Lousy Luke, Gruesome Gus, (Other Citizens), (Musicians), (Bartender), (Bank Teller)

NOTES: CITIZENS serve as narrators. For best effect, place CITIZENS 1 to 4 at far left, and 5 to 8 at far right, as seen from the audience. If possible, all readers should speak with a Western drawl. For special features, visit www.aaronshep.com/extras.

CITIZEN 1: Well, you've heard about gunfighting good guys like Wild Bill Hickok and Wyatt Earp.

CITIZEN 8: But we'll tell you a name that strikes even greater fear into the hearts of bad men everywhere.

ALL (except LARRY): Lightning Larry!

CITIZEN 2: We'll never forget the day Larry rode into our little town of Brimstone and walked into the Cottonmouth Saloon. He strode up to the bar and smiled straight at the bartender.

LIGHTNING LARRY: *(with a huge smile)* Lemonade, please!

CITIZEN 7: Every head in the place turned to look.

CITIZEN 3: Now, standing next to Larry at the bar was Crooked Curt.

CITIZEN 6: Curt was one of a band of rustlers and thieves that had been terrorizing our town, led by a ferocious outlaw named Evil-Eye McNeevil.

CITIZEN 4: Curt was wearing the usual outlaw scowl.

CITIZEN 5: Larry turned to him and smiled.

LIGHTNING LARRY: Mighty big frown you got there, mister!

CROOKED CURT: What's it to *you?*

LIGHTNING LARRY: Well, maybe I could help remove it!

CROOKED CURT: I'd like to see you try!

CITIZEN 1: The rest of us got out of the way real fast.

CITIZEN 8: The bartender ducked behind the bar.

CITIZEN 2: Larry and Curt moved about ten paces from each other, hands at the ready.

CITIZEN 7: Larry was still smiling.

CITIZEN 3: Curt moved first. But he only just cleared his gun from its holster before Larry aimed and fired.

LIGHTNING LARRY: *Zing!*

CITIZEN 6: There was no bang and no bullet. Just a little bolt of light that hit Curt right in the heart.

CITIZEN 4: Curt just stood there, his eyes wide with surprise. Then he dropped his gun, and a huge grin spread over his face.

CITIZEN 5: He rushed up to Larry and pumped his hand.

CROOKED CURT: I'm mighty glad to know you, stranger! The drinks are on me. Lemonade for everyone!

* * *

CITIZEN 1: When Evil-Eye McNeevil and his outlaw gang heard that Crooked Curt had gone straight, they shuddered right down to their boots.

CITIZEN 8: Most any outlaw would rather die than smile!

CITIZEN 2: Evil-Eye's men were shook up, but they weren't about to let on.

CITIZEN 7: The very next day,

DISMAL DAN: Dismal Dan!

DEVILISH DICK: Devilish Dick!

DREADFUL DAVE: And Dreadful Dave!

CITIZEN 7: rode into Brimstone, yelling like crazy men and shooting wild.

DAN, DICK, & DAVE: *(hoot and holler, prance, wave guns and shoot)*

CITIZEN 3: Windows shattered

CITIZEN 6: and citizens scattered.

CITIZEN 4: Then Lightning Larry showed up. He never warned them.

CITIZEN 5: Never even stopped smiling.

CITIZEN 1: Just shot three little bolts of light.

LIGHTNING LARRY: *Zing! Zing! Zing!*

DAN, DICK, & DAVE: *(stop and fall when hit)*

CITIZEN 8: Hit those outlaws right in the heart.

CITIZEN 2: Larry's shots knocked the outlaws to the ground. They lay there trying to figure out what had hit them. Then they got up and looked around.

DISMAL DAN: Looks like we did some damage, boys.

CITIZEN 7: . . . said Dismal Dan.

DEVILISH DICK: Hope nobody got hurt!

CITIZEN 3: . . . said Devilish Dick.

DREADFUL DAVE: We'd better get to work and fix this place up.

CITIZEN 6: . . . said Dreadful Dave.

CITIZEN 4: They spent the rest of the day replacing windows and apologizing to everyone who'd listen.

CITIZEN 5: Then for good measure, they picked up all the trash in the street.

* * *

CITIZEN 1: Evil-Eye McNeevil had lost three more of his meanest men,

CITIZEN 8: and he was furious!

CITIZEN 2: He decided to do something *really* nasty.

CITIZEN 7: The next day,

STINKY STEVE: Stinky Steve!

SICKENING SID: And Sickening Sid!

CITIZEN 7: walked into the 79th National Savings and Loan with guns in hand.

CITIZEN 3: They wore masks,

CITIZEN 6: but everyone knew who they were—from the smell.

STINKY STEVE: Stick up your hands.

CITIZEN 4: . . . said Stinky Steve.

SICKENING SID: Give us all the money in your vault.

CITIZEN 5: . . . ordered Sickening Sid.

CITIZEN 1: They were just backing out the door with the money bags, when Lightning Larry strolled by.

CITIZEN 8: Didn't even slow his step.

CITIZEN 2: Just shot those bandits in the back.

LIGHTNING LARRY: *Zing! Zing!*

CITIZEN 7: Went right through to the heart.

CITIZEN 3: The puzzled outlaws stopped and looked at each other.

STINKY STEVE: Seems a shame to steal the money of hardworking cowboys.

SICKENING SID: Wouldn't want to make their lives any harder.

CITIZEN 6: They holstered their guns and walked back to the teller.

CITIZEN 4: They plunked the money bags down on the counter.

SICKENING SID: Now, you keep that money safe.

CITIZEN 5: Then they pulled out their wallets and opened up accounts.

* * *

CITIZEN 1: That was the last straw for Evil-Eye McNeevil. It was time for a showdown!

CITIZEN 8: The next day at high noon, Larry was sipping lemonade at the Cottonmouth Saloon. Evil-Eye burst through the doors and stamped up to him.

EVIL-EYE McNEEVIL: I'm Evil-Eye McNeevil!

LIGHTNING LARRY: *(with a huge smile)* Hello, Evil-Eye! Can I buy you a lemonade?

EVIL-EYE McNEEVIL: This town ain't big enough for the both of us.

LIGHTNING LARRY: Seems pretty spacious to me!

EVIL-EYE McNEEVIL: I'll be waiting for you down by the Okey-Dokey Corral.

CITIZEN 8: And Evil-Eye stamped out.

CITIZEN 2: Larry finished his lemonade and walked out onto Main Street.

CITIZEN 7: Evil-Eye was waiting for him. But Evil-Eye wasn't alone.

CITIZEN 3: There on either side of him were

RAUNCHY RALPH: Raunchy Ralph!

GRIMY GREG: Grimy Greg!

CREEPY CAL: Creepy Cal!

MOLDY MIKE: Moldy Mike!

LOUSY LUKE: Lousy Luke!

GRUESOME GUS: And Gruesome Gus!

CITIZEN 6: And not a one of them looked friendly.

LIGHTNING LARRY: Nice day for a stroll!

CITIZEN 4: . . . called Larry.

EVIL-EYE McNEEVIL: Draw!

CITIZEN 5: . . . said Evil-Eye.

CITIZEN 1: All of us citizens of Brimstone were lining Main Street to see what would happen.

CITIZEN 8: Larry was still smiling, but we knew even Larry couldn't outshoot all those outlaws together.

CITIZEN 2: Just then a voice came from the Cottonmouth Saloon.

CROOKED CURT: Like some help, Larry?

LIGHTNING LARRY: Wouldn't mind it!

CITIZEN 7: Out stepped . . . Crooked Curt! And right behind him were Dismal Dan, Devilish Dick, Dreadful Dave, Stinky Steve, and Sickening Sid.

CITIZEN 3: They all took places beside Larry.

CROOKED CURT: Hello, Evil-Eye!

CITIZEN 6: . . . called Curt.

EVIL-EYE McNEEVIL: Traitors!

CITIZEN 4: . . . yelled Evil-Eye.

LIGHTNING LARRY: Draw!

CITIZEN 5: . . . said Larry, with a smile.

CITIZEN 1: Evil-Eye and his men drew their guns,

CITIZEN 8: but Larry and his friends were an eye-blink quicker.

CITIZEN 2: Their guns fired seven little bolts of light.

LARRY & FRIENDS: *Zing!*

CITIZEN 7: Hit those outlaws right in the you-know-what.

EVIL-EYE McNEEVIL: YIPPEE!

CITIZEN 3: . . . yelled Evil-Eye.

CITIZEN 6: He shot in the air.

EVIL-EYE McNEEVIL: *Zing!*

CITIZEN 4: There was no bang and no bullet.

CITIZEN 5: Just a little bolt of light.

LIGHTNING LARRY: All right, men! Let's clean up this town once and for all!

LARRY & ALL OUTLAWS: *(shoot at all others) Zing! Zing! Zing! . . .*

CITIZEN 1: And before we could duck for cover,

CITIZEN 8: Larry and Evil-Eye and the others

CITIZEN 2: turned their guns on the *rest* of us.

CITIZEN 7: Bolts of light flew everywhere.

CITIZEN 3: *No* one was spared—

CITIZEN 6: not a man,

CITIZEN 4: woman,

CITIZEN 5: or child!

ALL (except LARRY): YIPPEE!

CITIZEN 1: You never saw such a happy crowd!

CITIZEN 8: We all rushed around

CITIZEN 2: and pumped each other's hands

CITIZEN 7: and hugged each other.

CITIZEN 3: Then the musicians got out instruments and we had dancing too. Main Street was one huge party,

CITIZEN 6: all the rest of that day

CITIZEN 4: and on through the night.

CITIZEN 5: We never drank so much lemonade in all our days!

* * *

CITIZEN 1: With all the commotion, only a few of us saw Larry ride into the sunset.

CITIZEN 8: Can't say where he went.

CITIZEN 2: Can't say what he's doing now.

CITIZEN 7: But we bet he still aims for the heart.

ALL: *(shooting at audience) Zing!*

Mr. Bim's Bamboo

By Carol Farley

Adapted for reader's theater by Aaron Shepard, from Carol Farley's story in *Cricket* magazine, January 1989

> For more reader's theater, visit Aaron Shepard's RT Page at
> **www.aaronshep.com/rt**

PREVIEW: Mr. Bim's shop faces hard times when his customers turn to new things.

GENRE: Fantasy
CULTURE: East Asian (general)
THEME: Tradition vs. modernity

READERS: 8
READER AGES: 8–12
LENGTH: 6 minutes

ROLES: Narrators 1 & 2, Mr. Bim, Friend, Man, Boy, Women 1 & 2

NOTES: Bamboo, with its strength, rapid growth, and versatility, has a thousand traditional uses throughout East Asia. For a sample, see *Bamboo*, by Robert Austin, Koichiro Ueda, and Dana Levy. For best effect, place NARRATOR 1 at far left, and NARRATOR 2 at far right, as seen from the audience.

NARRATOR 1: Mr. Bim had a bamboo garden and a bamboo shop in a small village by a large mountain. He was old, and his face had more wrinkles than the mountain had trees. But he wore a shining white suit, and he always looked fine.

NARRATOR 2: His bamboo was fine too, and his shop was filled with useful things.

MR. BIM:

> I have bamboo trays and bamboo hats,
> Bamboo pots and bamboo mats.
> Bamboo frames and bamboo poles,
> Bamboo rugs and bamboo bowls.
>
> Try Bim's bamboo!

NARRATOR 1: People would hurry inside and buy.

FRIEND: Mr. Bim has the best bamboo in all the world!

NARRATOR 2: . . . they told each other, smiling and nodding and bowing. This made Mr. Bim feel so good, his head as he bowed nearly touched the ground.

NARRATOR 1: Then one morning, some people came from the other side of the mountain.

MR. BIM:

> I have the best, as you can see.
> Come and buy bamboo from me!

WOMAN 1: *(sneering)* Bim's bamboo. *Foo!*

NARRATOR 2: Mr. Bim's smile disappeared as quickly as a butterfly in a windstorm.

MAN: Bamboo is old! We want *new* things, *modern* things.

WOMAN 1: In *our* city, we buy *plastic.* Bim's bamboo. *Foo!*

MR. BIM: I've never heard of "plass-tick." Where does it grow?

MAN: Plastic doesn't grow! Plastic must be *made.*

WOMAN 1: *Nobody* wants *bamboo.* It's old and useless!

MAN: New things are always better!

NARRATOR 1: Soon all the people in the village were talking about the plastic from the other side of the mountain. *They* wanted plastic things, too. So they went to new shops.

NARRATOR 2: Mr. Bim's friend told him,

FRIEND: You must change your ways. You must become modern. Go over the mountain to the factories, and buy new things to sell in your shop.

MR. BIM: I am old like a turtle, and my ways are like a turtle shell— they make me what I am. Anyway, I don't think old things are always useless!

NARRATOR 1: As the months and years passed, Mr. Bim stayed near his quiet shop on the empty street.

NARRATOR 2: He took care of his lovely garden, kept his white coat and trousers shining, and dusted his beautiful bamboo. But no one came to buy.

NARRATOR 1: One day, after all the people had moved away from the small village, Mr. Bim stopped dusting his bamboo.

MR. BIM: It's foolish. No one will ever buy it again. Just like me, it's old and useless.

NARRATOR 2: Mr. Bim closed the door of his shop and sat down. He looked at the mountains far off in the distance.

NARRATOR 1: He saw that, in the wintertime, the mountaintops were covered with glistening white snow.

NARRATOR 2: Every spring, the snow melted into sparkling waterfalls.

NARRATOR 1: During the hot summer months, the water disappeared.

NARRATOR 2: But then, in late fall and winter, the snow came back to the mountaintops, glistening white and beautiful, the same as before.

NARRATOR 1: The old became new,

NARRATOR 2: and the new became old.

MR. BIM: *(thoughtfully, to himself)* I believe the mountains are trying to *tell* me something.

NARRATOR 1: Mr. Bim opened his shop door. Humming and smiling, he began dusting his beautiful bamboo.

NARRATOR 2: Just then, a little boy ran into the shop.

BOY: What's this?

NARRATOR 1: He picked up a bamboo whistle and blew it.

BOY: *(whistles)* Mommy! Come listen to this beautiful whistle!

NARRATOR 2: A young woman with travel bags hurried inside.

WOMAN 2: We must hurry on with the others. You have *many* whistles. You don't need another.

BOY: But this is different!

WOMAN 2: Different? *(looks around the shop)* My goodness! None of these things are plastic! *(to MR. BIM)* What are they made of?

MR. BIM: *(smiling)* Bamboo!

WOMAN 2: "Bam-boo"? I've never *heard* of it. Is it new?

MR. BIM: No, it's old!

WOMAN 2: What factory makes it?

MR. BIM: Bamboo grows! I have bamboo plants in my garden, and I made these bamboo things myself!

WOMAN 2: It *grows?* And you make all these beautiful things *yourself?* This is a miracle! *A miracle!*

MR. BIM: *(bowing)* The old is not always useless. The new is not always best.

WOMAN 2: I must tell the others about these treasures! *(to others outside)* Over here! Quickly! You must see this!

NARRATOR 1: Soon Mr. Bim's shop was full of people.

MAN: Beautiful!

WOMAN 1: A miracle!

MAN: And what do you suppose? Bamboo *grows!*

NARRATOR 2: As people began buying his bamboo, Mr. Bim smiled and nodded.

MR. BIM:

    I have bamboo trays and bamboo hats,
    Bamboo pots and bamboo mats.
    Bamboo frames and bamboo poles,
    Bamboo rugs and bamboo bowls.

    Some useful things are old.
    Some useful things are new.
    But what can be both old and new?

ALL:

    Bim's bam-boo!

Three Sideways Stories From Wayside School

By Louis Sachar

Adapted for reader's theater by Aaron Shepard, from Louis Sachar's book *Sideways Stories from Wayside School*, Avon, New York, 1985

For more reader's theater, visit Aaron Shepard's RT Page at
www.aaronshep.com/rt

PREVIEW: Some say the teachers and students at Wayside School are strange and silly—and so will you!

GENRE: Humor   READERS: 9
CULTURE: American   READER AGES: 8–12
THEME: Non-horizontal thinking   LENGTH: 12 minutes (1/2 + 3 + 4 + 4 + 1/2)

ROLES: Narrators 1–4, Mrs. Jewls, Joe, Bebe, Calvin, Louis

NOTES: Louis Sachar is the author of *Holes,* a Newbery Medal winner as well as the source of a major film. Other Wayside books by Sachar are *Wayside School Gets a Little Stranger* and *Wayside School Is Falling Down.* For best effect, place NARRATORS 1 and 2 at far left, and 3 and 4 at far right, as seen from the audience.

NARRATOR 1: We're going to tell you about three of the children in Mrs. Jewls's class, on the thirtieth story of Wayside School.

NARRATOR 4: But before we get to them, there is something you ought to know. Wayside School was accidentally built *sideways.*

NARRATOR 2: It was supposed to be only one story high, with thirty classrooms all in a row. Instead, it is *thirty* stories high, with one classroom on each *story.*

NARRATOR 3: The builder said he was very sorry.

NARRATOR 1: Our first story is about Joe. One day, Mrs. Jewls kept him in from recess.

MRS. JEWLS: Joe, you are going to have to learn to count.

JOE: But, Mrs. Jewls, I already *know* how to count. Let me go to recess!

MRS. JEWLS: First count to ten.

NARRATOR 4: Joe counted to ten.

JOE: Six, eight, twelve, one, five, two, seven, eleven, three, ten.

MRS. JEWLS: No, Joe, that is wrong.

JOE: No, it isn't! I counted till I got to ten!

MRS. JEWLS: But you were *wrong.* I'll *prove* it to you.

NARRATOR 2: She put down five pencils.

MRS. JEWLS: How many pencils do we have here, Joe?

NARRATOR 3: Joe counted the pencils.

JOE: Four, six, one, nine, five. There are five pencils, Mrs. Jewls.

MRS. JEWLS: That's *wrong.*

JOE: How many pencils *are* there?

MRS. JEWLS: Five.

JOE: That's what I said! May I go to recess now?

MRS. JEWLS: No. You got the right answer, but you counted the wrong *way.* You were just lucky.

NARRATOR 1: She set down eight potatoes.

MRS. JEWLS: How many potatoes, Joe?

NARRATOR 4: Joe counted the potatoes.

JOE: Seven, five, three, one, two, four, six, eight. There are eight potatoes, Mrs. Jewls.

MRS. JEWLS: No, there are *eight.*

JOE: But that's what I said! May I go to recess now?

MRS. JEWLS: No! You got the right answer, but you counted the wrong *way* again.

NARRATOR 2: She put down three books.

MRS. JEWLS: Count the books, Joe.

NARRATOR 3: Joe counted the books.

JOE: A thousand, a million, three. Three, Mrs. Jewls.

MRS. JEWLS: *(bewildered)* Correct.

JOE: May I go to recess now?

MRS. JEWLS: No.

JOE: May I have a potato?

MRS. JEWLS: No! *Listen* to me. One, two, three, four, five, six, seven, eight, nine, ten. Now *you* say it.

JOE: One, two, three, four, five, six, seven, eight, nine, ten.

MRS. JEWLS: Very good!

NARRATOR 1: She put down six erasers.

MRS. JEWLS: Now, count the erasers, Joe, just the way I showed you.

NARRATOR 4: Joe counted the erasers.

JOE: One, two, three, four, five, six, seven, eight, nine, ten. There are ten, Mrs. Jewls.

MRS. JEWLS: No!

JOE: Didn't I count right?

MRS. JEWLS: Yes, you *counted* right, but you got the wrong *answer.*

JOE: This doesn't make any sense! When I count the *wrong* way, I get the *right* answer, and when I count *right,* I get the *wrong* answer.

MRS. JEWLS: *(in great frustration) Ooh!*

NARRATOR 2: Mrs. Jewls hit her head against the wall five times.

MRS. JEWLS: *(turning away and butting her head)* Uh . . . uh . . . uh . . . uh . . . uh . . . . *(turns back to JOE)* How many times did I hit my head against the wall, Joe?

JOE: One, two, three, four, five, six, seven, eight, nine, ten. You hit your head against the wall ten times.

MRS. JEWLS: No!

JOE: Four, six, one, nine, five. You hit your head five times.

NARRATOR 3: Mrs. Jewls shook her head no and said,

MRS. JEWLS: *(shaking head)* Yes, that is right.

NARRATOR 1: Just then, the bell rang.

JOE: Oh, darn.

NARRATOR 4: . . . said Joe.

JOE: I missed recess!

_____

NARRATOR 3: Our second story is about Bebe.

NARRATOR 1: Bebe was the fastest draw in Mrs. Jewls's class. She could draw a cat in less than forty-five seconds, a dog in less than thirty, and a flower in less than eight seconds!

NARRATOR 4: But of course, Bebe never drew just *one* dog, or *one* cat, or *one* flower.

NARRATOR 2: Art was from 12:30 to 1:30. Why, in that time, she could draw fifty cats, a hundred flowers, twenty dogs, and several eggs or watermelons!

NARRATOR 3: You see, it took her the same time to draw a watermelon as an egg.

NARRATOR 1: Calvin sat next to Bebe. He didn't think he was very good at art. It took him the whole period just to draw one airplane.

NARRATOR 4: So instead, he just helped Bebe. He was Bebe's assistant.

NARRATOR 2: As soon as Bebe would finish one masterpiece, Calvin would take it from her and set down a clean sheet of paper. Whenever her crayon ran low, Calvin was ready with a new crayon.

NARRATOR 3: That way, Bebe didn't have to waste any time. And in return, Bebe would draw five or six airplanes for Calvin.

NARRATOR 1: It was 12:30, time for art.

NARRATOR 4: Bebe was ready. On her desk was a sheet of yellow construction paper. In her hand was a green crayon.

NARRATOR 2: *Calvin* was ready. He held a stack of paper and a box of crayons.

CALVIN: Ready, Bebe?

BEBE: Ready, Calvin.

MRS. JEWLS: All right, class.

NARRATOR 3: . . . said Mrs. Jewls.

MRS. JEWLS: Time for art.

NARRATOR 1: She had hardly finished her sentence when Bebe had drawn a picture of a leaf.

NARRATOR 4: Calvin took it from her and put down another piece of paper.

BEBE: Red!

NARRATOR 2: Calvin handed Bebe a red crayon.

BEBE: Blue!

NARRATOR 3: He gave her a blue crayon.

NARRATOR 1: They were quite a pair! Their teamwork was remarkable.

NARRATOR 4: Bebe drew pictures as fast as Calvin could pick up the old paper and set down the new.

NARRATOR 2: A fish.

NARRATOR 3: An apple.

NARRATOR 1: Three cherries—

NARRATOR 4: *bing,*

NARRATOR 2: *bing,*

NARRATOR 3: *bing.*

NARRATOR 1: At 1:30, Mrs. Jewls announced,

MRS. JEWLS: Okay, class, art is over.

NARRATOR 4: Bebe dropped her crayon and fell over on her desk.

NARRATOR 2: Calvin sighed and leaned back in his chair. He could hardly move.

NARRATOR 3: They had broken their old record. Bebe had drawn three hundred and seventy-eight pictures! They lay in a pile on Calvin's desk.

NARRATOR 1: Mrs. Jewls walked by.

MRS. JEWLS: Calvin, did you draw all these pictures?

CALVIN: No, *Bebe* drew them all.

MRS. JEWLS: Well then, what did *you* draw?

CALVIN: I didn't draw anything.

MRS. JEWLS: Why not? Don't you like art?

CALVIN: I *love* art. That's why I didn't draw anything.

MRS. JEWLS: I don't understand.

CALVIN: It would have taken me the whole period just to draw one picture. And *Bebe* would only have been able to draw a *hundred* pictures. But with the two of us working together, she was able to draw three hundred and seventy-eight pictures! That's a lot more art.

NARRATOR 4: Bebe and Calvin shook hands.

MRS. JEWLS: No, no! *That* isn't how you measure art. It isn't how *many* pictures you *have,* but how *good* the pictures *are.* Why, a person could spend their whole life drawing just one picture of a cat. In that time, I'm sure Bebe could draw a *million* cats.

BEBE: *Two* million.

MRS. JEWLS: But if that one picture is better than each of Bebe's two million, then that person has produced more art than Bebe.

NARRATOR 2: Bebe looked like she was going to cry. She picked up all the pictures from Calvin's desk and threw them in the garbage.

NARRATOR 3: Then she ran from the room, down all the stairs, and out onto the playground.

NARRATOR 1: Louis, the nice yard teacher, spotted her.

LOUIS: Where are you going, Bebe?

BEBE: I'm going home to draw a picture of a cat.

LOUIS: Will you bring it to school and show it to me tomorrow?

BEBE: *Tomorrow?* By *tomorrow* I doubt I'll be finished with even one *whisker. (rushes off)*

NARRATOR 2: Our final story is about Calvin. One day, Mrs. Jewls said,

MRS. JEWLS: Calvin, I want you to take this note to Miss Zarves for me.

CALVIN: Miss Zarves?

MRS. JEWLS: Yes, Miss Zarves. You know where she is, don't you?

CALVIN: Yes. She's on the nineteenth story.

MRS. JEWLS: That's right, Calvin. Take it to her.

NARRATOR 3: Calvin didn't move.

MRS. JEWLS: Well, what are you waiting for?

CALVIN: She's on the nineteenth story.

MRS. JEWLS: Yes, we have already established that fact.

CALVIN: The *nineteenth story.*

MRS. JEWLS: Yes, Calvin, the *nineteenth story.* Now take it to her before I lose my patience!

CALVIN: But, Mrs. Jewls—

MRS. JEWLS: NOW, Calvin!

CALVIN: Yes, ma'am!

NARRATOR 1: Calvin walked out of the classroom and stood outside the door.

NARRATOR 4: He didn't know where to go.

NARRATOR 2: As you know, when the builder built Wayside School, he accidentally built it sideways. But he also forgot to build the nineteenth *story.*

NARRATOR 3: He built the eighteenth and the twentieth, but no nineteenth. He said he was very sorry.

NARRATOR 1: There was also no Miss Zarves.

NARRATOR 4: Miss Zarves taught the class on the nineteenth story. Since there was no nineteenth story, there was no Miss Zarves.

NARRATOR 2: And besides *that,* as if Calvin didn't have enough problems, there was no note.

NARRATOR 3: Mrs. Jewls had never given Calvin the note.

CALVIN: *(sarcastically)* Boy, this is just great! I'm supposed to take a note that I don't have, to a teacher who doesn't exist, and who teaches on a story that was never built!

NARRATOR 1: He didn't know what to do.

NARRATOR 4: He walked down to the eighteenth story,

NARRATOR 2: then back up to the twentieth,

NARRATOR 3: then back down to the eighteenth,

NARRATOR 1: and back up again to the twentieth.

NARRATOR 4: There was no nineteenth story.

NARRATOR 2: There had never *been* a nineteenth story.

NARRATOR 3: There would never BE a nineteenth story.

NARRATOR 1: Calvin walked down to the administration office on the first story. He decided to put the note in Miss Zarves's mailbox.

NARRATOR 4: But there wasn't one of those, either. That didn't bother Calvin too much, though, since he didn't have a note.

NARRATOR 2: He looked out the window and saw Louis, the yard teacher, shooting baskets.

CALVIN: *Louis* will know what to do.

NARRATOR 3: Calvin went outside.

CALVIN: Hey, Louis!

LOUIS: Hi, Calvin. Do you want to play a game?

CALVIN: I don't have time. I have to deliver a note to Miss Zarves up on the nineteenth story.

LOUIS: Then what are you doing all the way down here?

CALVIN: There is no nineteenth story.

LOUIS: Then where is Miss Zarves?

CALVIN: There is no Miss Zarves.

LOUIS: What are you going to do with the note?

CALVIN: There is no note.

LOUIS: I understand.

CALVIN: That's good, because *I* sure don't.

LOUIS: It's very simple. You are not supposed to take no notes to no teachers. You already haven't done it!

NARRATOR 1: Calvin still didn't understand.

CALVIN: I'll just have to tell Mrs. Jewls that I couldn't deliver the note.

LOUIS: *That's* good. The truth is always best. Besides, I don't think *I* understand what I said, either!

NARRATOR 4: Calvin walked back up the thirty flights of stairs to Mrs. Jewls's class.

MRS. JEWLS: Thank you very much, Calvin.

CALVIN: But I—

MRS. JEWLS: That was a very important note, and I'm glad I was able to count on you.

CALVIN: Yes, but you see—

MRS. JEWLS: The note was very important. I told Miss Zarves *not* to meet me for lunch.

CALVIN: Don't worry.

NARRATOR 2: . . . said Calvin.

CALVIN: She won't!

NARRATOR 1: So now you know about Wayside School. Some people say these stories are strange and silly.

NARRATOR 4: That is probably true.

NARRATOR 2: But when the children at Wayside School heard stories about *us,* they thought *we* were strange and silly.

NARRATOR 3: And *that's* for *sure!*

The Jade Stone
A Chinese Folktale

Told by Caryn Yacowitz

Adapted for reader's theater by Aaron Shepard, from Caryn Yacowitz's picture book published by Holiday House, New York, 1992

For more reader's theater, visit Aaron Shepard's RT Page at
www.aaronshep.com/rt

PREVIEW: A stone carver must choose between obeying his emperor and obeying the stone he is given to carve.

GENRE: Folktales
CULTURE: Chinese (ancient)
THEME: Artistic process; artistic integrity
READERS: 11 or more
READER AGES: 8–12
LENGTH: 10 minutes

ROLES: Narrators 1–4, Chan Lo (male), Emperor, Stone, Advisers 1–3, Apprentice, (Emperor's Men/Guards)

NOTES: Jade is highly prized in China and often used there in sculpture. For best effect, place NARRATORS 1 and 2 at far left, and 3 and 4 at far right, as seen from the audience.

NARRATOR 1: Long ago in China there lived a stone carver named

CHAN LO: *(bowing)* Chan Lo.

NARRATOR 4: Chan Lo spent his days carving birds and deer and water buffalo from the colored stones he found near the river.

NARRATOR 2: His young apprentice asked,

APPRENTICE: How do you know what to carve?

CHAN LO: I always listen to the stone.

NARRATOR 3: . . . replied Chan Lo.

CHAN LO: The stone tells me what it wants to be.

NARRATOR 1: People came from near and far to buy Chan Lo's carvings.

NARRATOR 4: So it happened that when the Great Emperor of All China was given a perfect piece of green-and-white jade stone, one of the advisers in the Celestial Palace thought of

ADVISER 1: Chan Lo!

NARRATOR 2: The humble stone carver was brought before the Great Emperor of All China. Chan Lo bowed deeply.

EMPEROR: I want you to carve a dragon.

NARRATOR 3: . . . the emperor commanded.

EMPEROR: A dragon of wind and fire.

CHAN LO: I will do my best to please you.

NARRATOR 1: The emperor's men carried the precious stone to Chan Lo's garden.

NARRATOR 4: Chan Lo had never seen such a perfect piece of jade. The green-and-white of the stone was like moss-entangled-in-snow.

NARRATOR 2: The great emperor had commanded, "a dragon of wind and fire." Chan Lo wondered if that was what the stone wanted to be. He spoke to it.

CHAN LO:

> Here I stand, O Noble Stone,
> to carve a creature of your own.
> Whisper signs and sounds from rock
> that I, your servant, may unlock.

NARRATOR 3: Chan Lo bent down and put his ear to the stone. From deep inside came a gentle sound.

STONE: *(softly)* Pah-tah. Pah-tah. Pah-*tah.*

CHAN LO: Do dragons make that sound?

NARRATOR 1: . . . Chan Lo wondered.

CHAN LO: Perhaps the dragon's tail splashing in the ocean says, "Pah-tah, pah-*tah.*"

NARRATOR 4: But he was not sure.

NARRATOR 2: That evening, Chan Lo thought about dragons.

NARRATOR 3: But late at night, in his dreams, he heard,

STONE: Pah-tah. Pah-tah.

STONE & CHAN LO: Pah-*tah.*

NARRATOR 1: The next morning, Chan Lo went to the garden.

NARRATOR 4: The stone was spring-water-green in the morning light.

CHAN LO:

> Here I stand, O Noble Stone,
> to carve a creature of your own.
> Whisper signs and sounds from rock
> that I, your servant, may unlock.

NARRATOR 2: Chan Lo put his ear to the green-and-white jade and listened.

NARRATOR 3: Softly the sounds came.

STONE: *(softly)* Bub-bub-bubble. Bub-bub-bubble.

CHAN LO: Do dragons make that sound?

NARRATOR 1: . . . Chan Lo asked himself.

CHAN LO: Perhaps a dragon rising from the wild waves blows bubbles through his nostrils.

NARRATOR 4: But these were not mighty dragon bubbles that were coming from the rock. They were gentle, lazy, playful sounds.

NARRATOR 2: That evening, Chan Lo tried again to think about dragons.

NARRATOR 3: But when he went to bed, he heard in his dreams the sound of

STONE: Bub-bub-bubble. Bub-bub-bubble.

STONE & CHAN LO: Bub-bub-bubble.

NARRATOR 1: In the middle of the night, Chan Lo awoke. He walked into the moonlit garden.

NARRATOR 4: The stone shone silvery-green in the moonlight.

CHAN LO:

> Here I stand, O Noble Stone,
> to carve a creature of your own.
> Whisper signs and sounds from rock
> that I, your servant, may unlock.

NARRATOR 2: He put his ear to the stone. Silence.

NARRATOR 3: Chan Lo ran his hands over the jade. His fingers felt tiny ridges, and the ridges made a sound.

STONE: *(softly)* S-s-s-ah, S-s-s-s-s-ah, S-s-s-s-s-s-s-ah.

CHAN LO: Do dragons have ridges?

NARRATOR 1: . . . Chan Lo pondered.

CHAN LO: Yes. They have scales. Scales on their tails and bodies. And their scales *might* say, "S-s-s-ah, S-s-s-s-s-ah, S-s-s-s-s-s-s-ah," if one dared to touch them.

NARRATOR 4: But Chan Lo knew these small, delicate ridges were *not* dragon scales.

NARRATOR 2: Chan Lo could not carve what he did not hear, but he was afraid to disobey the emperor.

NARRATOR 3: His fear weighed in him like a great stone as he picked up his tools and began to carve.

* * *

NARRATOR 1: Chan Lo worked slowly and carefully for a year and a day.

NARRATOR 4: Finally, the carving was complete.

NARRATOR 2: Early in the morning, before the birds were awake, Chan Lo and his apprentice wrapped the jade carving in a cloth and set out for the Celestial Palace.

NARRATOR 3: Chan Lo entered the Great Hall, where the three advisers sat waiting for the Great Emperor of All China. He placed the jade stone on the table in the center of the room.

NARRATOR 1: Soon the emperor's advisers grew curious. They scurried to the jade stone and peeked under the cloth.

ADVISER 1: *(surprised)* No dragon!

ADVISER 2: *(louder) No dragon!*

ADVISER 3: *(loudest)* NO DRAGON!

NARRATOR 4: At that moment, the emperor himself entered the Great Hall.

EMPEROR: Show me my dragon of wind and fire!

NARRATOR 2: The advisers whisked the cloth away.

EMPEROR: *(thundering) This* is not my dragon!

ADVISER 1: *(pointing at CHAN LO)* Punish him!

ADVISER 2: *Punish him!*

ADVISER 3: PUNISH HIM!

NARRATOR 3: Chan Lo's knees shook like ginkgo leaves in the wind.

CHAN LO: O mighty emperor, there *is* no dragon of wind and fire. I did not *hear* it! I heard these three carp fish swimming playfully in the reeds in the pool of the Celestial Palace.

EMPEROR: *Hear* them? You did not *hear* them!

ADVISER 1: Chop off his head!

ADVISER 2: *Boil him in oil!*

ADVISER 3: CUT HIM IN A THOUSAND PIECES!

NARRATOR 1: But the emperor was so angry, he could not decide which punishment to choose.

EMPEROR: I will let my *dreams* decide his punishment. Now, take him away! And remove that stone from the Celestial Palace!

NARRATOR 4: Chan Lo was dragged down many flights of stairs and thrown into a black prison cell. The carving was placed outside, near the reeds of the reflecting pool.

* * *

NARRATOR 2: That evening, the emperor thought about dragons.

NARRATOR 3: But late that night, in his sleep, the emperor dreamed of fish playfully slapping their tails in green water.

STONE: Pah-tah. Pah-tah.

STONE & EMPEROR: Pah-*tah.*

NARRATOR 1: In the morning, the emperor's advisers asked,

ADVISER 1: What punishment have you chosen?

NARRATOR 4: But the emperor said,

EMPEROR: My dreams have not yet decided.

NARRATOR 2: That evening, the emperor again tried to think about dragons.

NARRATOR 3: But when he went to bed, the emperor dreamed of fish gliding smoothly through deep, clear water.

STONE: Bub-bub-bubble. Bub-bub-bubble.

STONE & EMPEROR: Bub-bub-bubble.

NARRATOR 1: In the morning, the emperor's advisers again asked him,

ADVISER 2: What punishment have your dreams chosen?

NARRATOR 4: But the emperor told them,

EMPEROR: My dreams have still not decided.

NARRATOR 2: On the third night, the emperor groaned and tossed in his sleep, but he did not dream.

NARRATOR 3: He awoke in the darkest hour of the night. A strange sound filled the room.

STONE: S-s-s-ah, S-s-s-s-s-ah, S-s-s-s-s-s-s-ah.

NARRATOR 1: The emperor got out of bed and went toward the sound. He hurried down the corridors, through the Great Hall, and out into the moonlit garden.

NARRATOR 4: There by the reflecting pool was the jade stone. Next to it stood the apprentice, running his fingers down the scales of the three carp fish.

STONE: S-s-s-ah, S-s-s-s-s-ah, S-s-s-s-s-s-s-ah.

NARRATOR 2: When the apprentice had gone, the emperor sat near the pool and gazed at the jade stone. The shining scales of the jade carp glowed in the moonlight. The fishes' slippery bodies were reflected in the pool. They seemed ready to flick their tails and swim among the reeds.

NARRATOR 3: The emperor remained by the pool until his advisers found him at sunrise.

ADVISER 3: What punishment have your dreams chosen?

EMPEROR: *(smiling)* Bring Chan Lo before me.

* * *

NARRATOR 1: Chan Lo bowed deeply before the Great Emperor of All China, ready to receive his terrible punishment.

EMPEROR: You have disobeyed me, Chan Lo, but you are a brave man to defy the Great Emperor of All China. You have carved the creatures that were in the stone. I, too, have heard them. These three carp fish are dearer to me than any dragon of wind and fire. What reward would you have?

CHAN LO: *(grateful and relieved, bowing even lower)* Great Emperor, your happiness with my work is my reward. I wish only to return to my village and carve what I hear.

EMPEROR: You *will* carve what you hear. And you will return to your village in great honor—as befits the Master Carver to the Great Emperor of All China!

STONE: Pah-*tah!*

Talk

Told by Harold Courlander

Adapted for reader's theater by Aaron Shepard, from Harold Courlander's story in his and George Herzog's book *The Cow-Tail Switch, and Other West African Stories,* Holt, New York, 1947

For more reader's theater, visit Aaron Shepard's RT Page at
www.aaronshep.com/rt

PREVIEW: A farmer's day goes awry when he gets lip from a yam.

GENRE: Tall tales, folktales
CULTURE: African (western), Ashanti
THEME: Predictability

READERS: 15 or more
READER AGES: 8–15
LENGTH: 4 minutes

ROLES: Narrators 1 & 2, Yam, Dog, Tree, Branch, Stone, Fisherman, Trap, Weaver, Cloth, Bather, River, Chief, Stool, (Cow)

NOTES: Harold Courlander heard this story in Nigeria, told by an Ashanti from Ghana. For best effect, place NARRATOR 1 at far left, and NARRATOR 2 at far right, as seen from the audience. Each talking animal or object should have a distinctive funny voice, and the human characters should imitate them while describing what they said. *Wah* is a common African exclamation.

NARRATOR 1: Once, not far from the city of Accra, a man went out to his garden to dig up some yams to take to market. While he was digging, one of the yams said to him,

YAM: So, you're finally here! You never weeded me, but now you come around with your digging stick. Go away and *leave me alone!*

NARRATOR 2: The farmer turned around and looked at his cow in amazement. The cow was chewing her cud and looking at *him.*

FARMER: Did you *say* something?

NARRATOR 2: The cow kept chewing and said nothing. But the man's *dog* spoke up.

DOG: It wasn't the cow who spoke to you. It was the yam! The yam says leave him alone!

NARRATOR 1: The man became angry, because his dog had never talked before, and he didn't like its tone, besides. So he took his knife and cut a branch from a palm tree to whip his dog. But then the *palm* tree said,

TREE: Put that branch down!

NARRATOR 2: The man was getting upset. He was just about to throw the branch away, when the *branch* said,

BRANCH: Man, put me down softly!

NARRATOR 1: He put the branch down gently on a stone. But the *stone* said,

STONE: Hey! Take that thing off me!

FARMER: *(freaking out)* WAH!

NARRATOR 2: The frightened farmer started to run for his village. On the way, he met a fisherman carrying along a fish trap on his head.

FISHERMAN: What's the hurry?

FARMER: The yam said, "Leave me alone!" The dog said, "Listen to the yam!" The tree said, "Put that branch down!" The branch said, "Do it softly!" And the stone said, "Take that thing off me!"

FISHERMAN: Is that all? Is that so frightening?

TRAP: Well?

NARRATOR 2: . . . said the man's fish trap.

TRAP: Did he take the branch off the stone?

FARMER & FISHERMAN: WAH!

NARRATOR 1: The fisherman threw down the fish trap and began to run with the farmer. On the trail, they met a weaver with a bundle of cloth on his head.

WEAVER: Why are you in such a rush?

FARMER: The yam said, "Leave me alone!" The dog said, "Listen to the yam!" The tree said, "Put that branch down!" The branch said, "Do it softly!" The stone said, "Take that thing off me!"

FISHERMAN: And the trap said, "Did he take it off?"

WEAVER: *That's* nothing to get excited about. No reason at all!

CLOTH: Oh, yes, it is!

NARRATOR 1: . . . said the bundle of cloth.

CLOTH: If it happened to *you,* you'd run too!

FARMER, FISHERMAN, & WEAVER: WAH!

NARRATOR 2: The weaver threw down his bundle and ran with the other men. They came panting to the ford in the river, and found a man taking a bath.

BATHER: Why are you running like that? Are you chasing a gazelle?

FARMER: The yam said, "Leave me alone!" The dog said, "Listen to the yam!" The tree said, "Put that branch down!" The branch said, "Do it softly!" The stone said, "Take that thing off me!"

FISHERMAN: The trap said, "Did he take it off?"

WEAVER: And the cloth said, "You'd run too!"

BATHER: And that made you run?

RIVER: Well, why not?

NARRATOR 2: . . . said the river.

RIVER: Wouldn't *you* run, if it were you?

FARMER, FISHERMAN, WEAVER, & BATHER: WAH!

NARRATOR 1: The man jumped naked out of the water and began to run with the others. They ran into the village and down the main street, till they reached the house of the chief.

NARRATOR 2: The chief brought out his royal stool and sat on it to listen to their complaints. The men began to recite their troubles.

FARMER: I went out to my garden to dig yams. Then everything began to talk! The yam said, "Leave me alone!" The dog said, "Listen to the yam!" The tree said, "Put that branch down!" The branch said, "Do it softly!" The stone said, "Take that thing off me!"

FISHERMAN: The trap said, "Did he take it off?"

WEAVER: The cloth said, "You'd run too!"

BATHER: And the river said, "Wouldn't you?"

NARRATOR 1: The chief listened patiently at first, but finally grew annoyed.

CHIEF: Now, this is a really wild story. Go back to your work, *all* of you, before I punish you for disturbing the peace!

FARMER, FISHERMAN, WEAVER, BATHER: *(back off fearfully and leave)*

NARRATOR 2: So the men went away. The chief shook his head.

CHIEF: That kind of nonsense upsets the community.

STOOL: Ridiculous, isn't it!

NARRATOR 2: . . . said his royal stool.

STOOL: Imagine! A talking yam!

CHIEF: WAH!

The Bean Boy

By Monica Shannon

Adapted for reader's theater by Aaron Shepard, from Monica Shannon's story in her book *California Fairy Tales,* Doubleday, New York, 1926

> For more reader's theater, visit Aaron Shepard's RT Page at
> **www.aaronshep.com/rt**

PREVIEW: A farm boy with wayward shoelaces offers to find the dream of the Governor's daughter.

GENRE: Fantasy   READERS: 8–10
CULTURE: Californian (Spanish colonial),   READER AGES: 9–12
   Irish-American   LENGTH: 8 minutes
THEME: Determination; helpfulness

ROLES: Narrators 1–4, Bean Boy, Dulce (female), Goblin, Sandman, Governor, Soldier

NOTES: In this original "California fairy tale," Monica Shannon draws on both the Spanish colonial heritage of California, and her own Irish heritage. For best effect, place NARRATORS 1 and 2 at far left, and 3 and 4 at far right, as seen from the audience. GOBLIN can double as GOVERNOR, and SANDMAN can double as SOLDIER.

NARRATOR 1: In the years between this and that, there lived a boy named String,

NARRATOR 4: because he used strings for shoelaces—

BEAN BOY: *(pointing to each shoe)* A red string in one shoe, and a green string in the other.

NARRATOR 2: Now, String lived in a lima bean field. And when the lima beans were green, he picked them, put them in sacks, and took sackfuls of green lima beans into town to sell.

NARRATOR 3: So he was called the Bean Boy.

NARRATOR 1: One morning, String the Bean Boy started off for the governor's palace with a sack of green lima beans. The governor's daughter had ordered large, flat beans for her soup.

NARRATOR 4: She was called Dulce because, although her eyes were dark and sad, her smile was as sweet and gaudy as the red seaweed, dulce.

NARRATOR 2: Now, Dulce was leaning out of the palace window, watching for her sack of large, flat beans. The Bean Boy came whistling into the patio of the palace, tripping over his shoestrings—

BEAN BOY: *(trips, then points)* A red string, and a green string.

NARRATOR 2: always coming undone.

NARRATOR 3: Dulce ran downstairs, fetching a pan, so the Bean Boy could dump out his sack of big, flat beans. Then the Bean Boy sat down to tie up his green and red shoestrings.

NARRATOR 1: By this time, the governor's daughter had stopped smiling, so String noticed how sad and dark her eyes looked. The girl said,

DULCE: It must be nice to live in a bean field and bring sacks of beans into town.

BEAN BOY: It *is* nice. And I am always finding things on my way in and out.

DULCE: What *kind* of things?

BEAN BOY: Oh, tree toads, and moonstones, and old Spanish coins, and Indian beads, and kelp for dress-up helmets!

NARRATOR 4: The governor's daughter smiled her gaudy smile.

DULCE: Maybe . . . maybe you can find my dream for me?

BEAN BOY: Maybe I can!

DULCE: I dreamed that my father was not a governor any more, and he didn't need to worry about revolutions. I dreamed he was an organ-grinder man, with a tiny tomboy monkey from Central America.

BEAN BOY: *(encouragingly) I* know. And you went with him, walking through bean fields, singing "Ma-*ri*-a *Mi*-a." And people filled your cup with pennies. And you made a bonfire every night and popped corn.

DULCE: Yes! Yes! And my father didn't worry any more about revolutions. Just think, he didn't need to worry about revolutions!

NARRATOR 2: Dulce opened her sad eyes wide open.

DULCE: But I only dreamed it once. Now, do you think you can find my dream again for me?

BEAN BOY: Of course! I can find *anything* on my way in and out.

DULCE: Then I mean to marry you when you grow up tall!

NARRATOR 3: At that, the Bean Boy went whistling away, tripping over his shoestrings—

BEAN BOY: *(trips, then points)* A red string, and a green string. *(goes off whistling)*

NARRATOR 3: always coming undone.

* * *

NARRATOR 1: Next morning at sunup, String the Bean Boy was picking big, flat beans and putting them into sacks, when a Goblin came hurrying up a bean row. The Goblin tipped his bean-leaf cap and inquired politely,

GOBLIN: Could you possibly spare two good-sized beans this morning? The finest baby of our king will be christened in sixteen minutes, and I find myself without a christening present.

NARRATOR 4: The polite Goblin bowed as best he could, for he was a thick little person. He had a wide, cheerful mouth, and looked hearty in his seaweed suit.

BEAN BOY: Fill your cap!

NARRATOR 2: . . . String told him, and he helped the Goblin pick eight or ten fine lima beans. Then he said in a hurry,

BEAN BOY: While you are here, I wish you would tell me where to find the dream of the governor's daughter, Dulce.

GOBLIN: *(bows)* Certainly. All dreams are kept in the Cave of Yawns, down by the sea—two leagues south, two leagues west. But remember not to yawn in the cave! Every time anyone yawns, the cave gets bigger. And if you go to sleep in there, you will never wake up.

NARRATOR 3: Then the Goblin hurried off to the king's baby's christening.

NARRATOR 1: The Bean Boy hurried off too, going two leagues south, two leagues west.

NARRATOR 4: And there he was, down by the sea, at the Cave of Yawns.

NARRATOR 2: There were dark chests along the cave walls—rich, hand-carved chests, from which the Sandman was selecting dreams.

NARRATOR 3: The Sandman stood at the farthest end of the cave, throwing a handful of sand into his bag and then a dream, a handful of sand and then a dream.

NARRATOR 1: The Bean Boy called out,

BEAN BOY: Sandman!

NARRATOR 4: But when the Sandman looked up, the Bean Boy yawned. The cave got bigger, just as the polite Goblin had said it would. The Sandman was leagues farther away now.

NARRATOR 2: The Bean Boy began to feel sleepy.

NARRATOR 3: His hands went to sleep, his feet went to sleep, and every step pricked like pins and needles.

NARRATOR 1: Then the Bean Boy yawned again, and the cave got bigger, just as the polite Goblin had said it would. The Sandman and the rich, hand-carved chests were so far away now, they looked like dots on a dotted line.

NARRATOR 4: Then the Bean Boy's ears went to sleep. After that, his nose went to sleep. But he said to himself,

BEAN BOY: *(sleepily)* Even though I feel all over like a pincushion, I must keep my two eyes awake and walk with my feet asleep, till I can nudge the Sandman and get Dulce's dream for her.

NARRATOR 2: So the Bean Boy walked with his feet asleep, his hands asleep, his ears asleep, and his nose asleep. But the jolt of tripping over his shoestrings kept his eyes awake, until he nudged the Sandman.

NARRATOR 3: The Bean Boy stifled an enormous yawn.

BEAN BOY: *(making faces, talking slow and funny, as he struggles not to yawn)* Please, may I have Dulce's dream?

SANDMAN: What was it like? And about how long?

BEAN BOY: Hurry! I'm going to yawn again!

SANDMAN: *(searching in a chest)* Did it have a monkey and an organ grinder in it? And a song that goes, "Ma-*ri*-a *Mi*-a?"

BEAN BOY: *(still struggling)* Yes! Yes!

NARRATOR 1: The Bean Boy's eyes were closing. But he tripped over his shoestrings and opened his eyes again with a terrible effort.

SANDMAN: *(holds the dream up like a piece of clothing, looks it up and down)* It's an *old* dream, almost worn out. So I suppose you may as well have it.

NARRATOR 4: The Sandman shook the dream out, sticking his finger through the holes. Then he handed over the tattered dream.

NARRATOR 2: The Bean Boy ran from the cave with his feet asleep, his hands asleep, his ears asleep, and his nose asleep.

NARRATOR 3: He was really asleep all over, except that his eyes were awake from the jolt of tripping over his shoestrings—

BEAN BOY: *(trips, then points, still struggling not to yawn)* A red string in one shoe . . . and a green string in the other. *(runs off)*

* * *

NARRATOR 1: Next morning before dawn, the boy started for town with his bean sacks and the old dream, which looked as if it were falling to pieces.

NARRATOR 4: When he came near the gates of the town, he heard guns! Soldiers came out, singing,

NARRATORS 1, 2, 3, & 4: Ma-*ri*-a *Mi*-a!

NARRATOR 2: The Bean Boy went into town. The palace was in ruins, and there on some stones sat the governor and Dulce. The Bean Boy noticed how sad and dark her eyes were.

GOVERNOR: It is just what I worried about!

NARRATOR 4: . . . moaned the governor. And Dulce told the Bean Boy,

DULCE: We have had another revolution.

NARRATOR 2: Just then, a soldier came running up and spoke low to the governor.

SOLDIER: Your Excellency must go away at once in disguise!

GOVERNOR: *(hopelessly)* Where can I go? What can I do?

NARRATOR 3: Whereupon the Bean Boy handed him the old, worn dream.

GOVERNOR: *(puts on the dream and becomes an organ-grinder)*

* * *

NARRATOR 1: And so it happened that the governor disguised himself as an organ-grinder man, owning a tiny tomboy monkey from Central America.

NARRATOR 4: He and Dulce and String the Bean Boy wandered up and down the world joyously, making bonfires every night and popping corn.

NARRATOR 2: After they had wandered from one end of the world to the other, the Bean Boy married Dulce one night by a big campfire,

NARRATOR 3: and they inherited great stretches of bean fields,

NARRATOR 1: where they lived happily,

NARRATOR 4: for years,

NARRATOR 2: and years,

NARRATOR 3: and years,

BEAN BOY & DULCE: and years.

How Tom Beat Captain Najork

By Russell Hoban

Adapted for reader's theater by Aaron Shepard, from Russell Hoban's picture book *How Tom Beat Captain Najork and His Hired Sportsmen*, Atheneum, New York, 1974

For more reader's theater, visit Aaron Shepard's RT Page at
www.aaronshep.com/rt

PREVIEW: Tom won't stop fooling around, so his aunt sends for Captain Najork to teach that boy a lesson.

GENRE: Humor   READERS: 10
CULTURE: British   READER AGES: 9–13
THEME: Value of play   LENGTH: 10 minutes

ROLES: Narrators 1 & 2, Tom, Aunt Fidget, Captain Najork, Sportsmen 1–4, Aunt Bundlejoy

NOTES: For best effect, place NARRATOR 1 at far left, and NARRATOR 2 at far right, as seen from the audience. AUNT FIDGET and CAPTAIN NAJORK are meant to be "very British."

NARRATOR 1: Tom lived with his maiden aunt, Miss Fidget Wonkham-Strong. She wore an iron hat and took no nonsense from anyone. Where she walked, the flowers drooped. When she sang, the trees all shivered.

NARRATOR 2: Tom liked to fool around. He fooled around with sticks and stones and crumpled paper,

NARRATOR 1: with mewses and passages and dustbins,

NARRATOR 2: with bent nails and broken glass and holes in fences.

NARRATOR 1: He fooled around with mud, and stomped and squelched and slithered through it.

NARRATOR 2: He fooled around on high-up things that shook and wobbled and teetered.

NARRATOR 1: He fooled around with dropping things off bridges into rivers and fishing them out.

NARRATOR 2: He fooled around with barrels in alleys.

NARRATOR 1: When Aunt Fidget Wonkham-Strong asked,

AUNT FIDGET: Tom! What are you doing?

NARRATOR 2: Tom said,

TOM: Fooling around.

AUNT FIDGET: It looks very like *playing* to *me.* Too much playing is not good, and you play too much. You had better stop it and do something useful.

TOM: All right.

NARRATOR 2: But he did *not* stop. He did a little fooling around with three cigar bands and a paper clip.

NARRATOR 1: At dinner, Aunt Fidget Wonkham-Strong, wearing her iron hat, said,

AUNT FIDGET: Eat your mutton and your cabbage-and-potato sog.

TOM: All right.

NARRATOR 2: He ate it.

NARRATOR 1: After dinner, Aunt Fidget Wonkham-Strong said,

AUNT FIDGET: Now learn off pages 65 to 75 of the *Nautical Almanac.* That will teach you not to fool around so much.

TOM: All right.

NARRATOR 2: He learned them off.

AUNT FIDGET: From now on, I shall keep an eye on you. If you do not stop fooling around, I shall send for Captain Najork and his hired sportsmen!

TOM: Who is Captain Najork?

AUNT FIDGET: Captain Najork is seven feet tall, with eyes like fire, a voice like thunder, and a handlebar mustache. His trousers are always freshly pressed, his blazer is immaculate, his shoes are polished mirror-bright, and he is every inch a terror.

When Captain Najork is sent for, he comes up the river in his pedal boat, with his hired sportsmen all pedaling hard. He teaches fooling-around boys the lesson they so badly need—and it is not one they soon forget!

NARRATOR 1: Aunt Fidget Wonkham-Strong kept an eye on Tom.

NARRATOR 2: But he did not stop fooling around.

NARRATOR 1: He did low and muddy fooling around.

NARRATOR 2: He did high and wobbly fooling around.

NARRATOR 1: He fooled around with dropping things off bridges.

NARRATOR 2: And he fooled around with barrels in alleys.

AUNT FIDGET: Very well.

NARRATOR 1: . . . said Aunt Fidget Wonkham-Strong, sitting at table in her iron hat.

AUNT FIDGET: Eat your greasy bloaters.

NARRATOR 2: Tom ate them.

AUNT FIDGET: I have warned you that I should send for Captain Najork if you did not stop fooling around. I have done that. As you like to play so much, you shall play against Captain Najork and his hired sportsmen. They play hard games, and they play them jolly hard. Prepare yourself!

TOM: All right. *(fools around some more)*

* * *

NARRATOR 1: The next day, Captain Najork came up the river, with his hired sportsmen pedaling his pedal boat.

NARRATOR 2: They came ashore smartly, carrying an immense brown-paper parcel.

NARRATOR 1: They marched into the garden.

SPORTSMAN 1: One!

SPORTSMAN 2: Two!

SPORTSMAN 3: Three!

SPORTSMAN 4: Four!

NARRATOR 2: Captain Najork was only six feet tall. His eyes were not like fire. His voice was not like thunder.

CAPTAIN: Right!

NARRATOR 1: . . . said Captain Najork.

CAPTAIN: Where *is* the sportive infant?

AUNT FIDGET: *(points)* There.

NARRATOR 1: . . . said Aunt Fidget Wonkham-Strong.

TOM: *(raises hand)* Here!

NARRATOR 2: . . . said Tom.

CAPTAIN: Right! We shall play womble, muck, and sneedball—in that order.

NARRATOR 1: The hired sportsmen sniggered as they undid the immense brown-paper parcel and set up

SPORTSMAN 1: The womble run!

SPORTSMAN 2: The ladders!

SPORTSMAN 3: The net!

SPORTSMAN 4: The rakes!

SPORTSMAN 1: The stakes!

TOM: How do you play womble?

CAPTAIN: *(smirking) You'll* find out.

TOM: Who's on *my* side?

CAPTAIN: Nobody! Let's get started!

NARRATOR 2: Womble turned out to be a shaky, high-up, wobbling and teetering sort of game, and Tom was used to that kind of fooling around.

NARRATOR 1: The Captain's side raked first.

NARRATOR 2: Tom staked.

NARRATOR 1: The hired sportsmen played so hard that they wombled too fast and were shaky with the rakes.

NARRATOR 2: Tom fooled around the way he always did, and all his stakes dropped true.

NARRATOR 1: When it was Tom's turn to rake, he did not let Captain Najork and the hired sportsmen score a single rung.

NARRATOR 2: At the end of the snetch, he had won by six ladders!

CAPTAIN: *(clenching his teeth)* Right!

NARRATOR 1: . . . said Captain Najork.

CAPTAIN: Muck next. Same sides.

SPORTSMEN 1, 2, 3, & 4: *(snigger)*

NARRATOR 1: The court was laid out at low tide in the river mud.

NARRATOR 2: Tom mucked first and slithered through the marks, while the hired sportsmen poled and shoveled. Tom had fooled around with mud so much that he scored time after time.

NARRATOR 1: Captain Najork's men poled too hard and shoveled too fast, and tired themselves out.

NARRATOR 2: Tom just mucked about and fooled around. When the tide came in, he led the opposition 673 to 49!

AUNT FIDGET: *(distressed)* Really!

NARRATOR 1: . . . said Aunt Fidget Wonkham-Strong to Captain Najork.

AUNT FIDGET: You must make an effort to teach this boy a lesson!

CAPTAIN: Some boys learn hard.

NARRATOR 2: . . . said the Captain, chewing his mustache.

CAPTAIN: Now for sneedball!

NARRATOR 1: The hired sportsmen brought out

SPORTSMAN 2: The ramp!

SPORTSMAN 3: The slide!

SPORTSMAN 4: The barrel!

SPORTSMAN 1: The bobble!

SPORTSMAN 2: The tongs!

SPORTSMAN 3: The bar!

SPORTSMAN 4: The grapples!

NARRATOR 2: Tom saw at once that sneedball was like several kinds of fooling around he was particularly good at. Partly it was like dropping things off bridges into rivers and fishing them out, and partly it was like fooling around with barrels in alleys.

CAPTAIN: I had better tell you

NARRATOR 1: . . . said the Captain to Tom,

CAPTAIN: that I played in the Sneedball Finals, five years running.

TOM: They couldn't have been very final, if you had to keep doing it for five years!

NARRATOR 2: He motioned the Captain aside, away from Aunt Fidget Wonkham-Strong.

TOM: *(in a low voice)* Let's make this interesting.

CAPTAIN: *(also in a low voice)* What do you mean?

TOM: Let's play *for* something. Let's say, if I win, I get your pedal boat.

CAPTAIN: What do I get if *I* win? Because I am certainly going to win *this* one.

TOM: You can have Aunt Fidget Wonkham-Strong!

CAPTAIN: Hmm. She's impressive. I admit that freely. A very *impressive* lady.

TOM: She fancies you. I can tell by the way she looks at you sideways from beneath her iron hat.

CAPTAIN: No!

TOM: Yes!

CAPTAIN: And you'll *part* with her, if she'll *have* me?

TOM: It's the only sporting thing to do!

CAPTAIN: *(loudly again)* Agreed, then! *(shakes hands on it)* By George! I'm almost sorry I'll have to *teach* you a lesson by beating you at sneedball!

TOM: Let's get started!

CAPTAIN: Right!

NARRATOR 1: The hired sportsmen had first slide. Captain Najork himself barreled, and he and his men played like demons.

NARRATOR 2: But Tom tonged the bobble in the same fooling-around way he fished things out of rivers, and he quickly moved into the lead.

NARRATOR 1: Captain Najork sweated big drops, and he slid his barrel too hard, so it hit the stop and slopped over.

NARRATOR 2: But Tom just fooled around. When it was his slide, he never spilled a drop.

NARRATOR 1: Darkness fell, but they shot up flares and went on playing.

NARRATOR 2: By three o'clock in the morning, Tom had *won*—

NARRATOR 1: 85 to 10!

NARRATOR 2: As the last flare went up over the garden, Tom looked down from the ramp at the defeated Captain and his hired sportsmen.

TOM: Maybe that will teach you not to fool around with a boy who knows how to fool around!

CAPTAIN: *(starts bawling)*

NARRATOR 1: Captain Najork broke down and wept, but Aunt Fidget Wonkham-Strong put him to bed and brought him peppermint tea, and then he felt better.

NARRATOR 2: Tom took his new boat and pedaled to the next town down the river. There he advertised in the newspaper for a new aunt. When he found one he liked, he told her,

TOM: *(firmly)* No greasy bloaters, no mutton, and no cabbage-and-potato sog. No *Nautical Almanac.* And I do lots of fooling around. Those are my conditions.

AUNT BUNDLEJOY: *(giggles)*

NARRATOR 1: The new aunt's name was Bundlejoy Cosysweet.

NARRATOR 2: She had a floppy hat with flowers on it, and long, long hair.

AUNT BUNDLEJOY: That sounds fine to me! We'll have a go.

NARRATOR 1: Aunt Fidget Wonkham-Strong married Captain Najork—

NARRATOR 2: even though he *had* lost the sneedball game—

NARRATOR 1: and they were very happy together.

NARRATOR 2: She made the hired sportsmen learn off pages of the *Nautical Almanac* every night—

NARRATOR 1 & 2: after dinner.

SPORTSMEN 1, 2, 3, & 4: Yuck!

Tapiwa's Uncle

By Nancy Farmer

Adapted for reader's theater by Aaron Shepard, from Nancy Farmer's story in *Cricket* magazine, February 1992

> For more reader's theater, visit Aaron Shepard's RT Page at
> **www.aaronshep.com/rt**

PREVIEW: When Uncle Zeka arrives in the city from his village, his attempts to be helpful don't always work out.

GENRE: Humor
CULTURE: African (southeastern)
THEME: Cultural diversity

READERS: 7 or more
READER AGES: 9–13
LENGTH: 10 minutes

ROLES: Narrators 1 & 2, Tapiwa (female), Tongai (male), Father, Mother, Uncle Zeka, (Police), (Firemen), (House Owners)

NOTES: This story and others about Uncle Zeka became Nancy Farmer's first book in the U.S., *Do You Know Me*. The stories are based on her experiences in Zimbabwe, where she lived and wrote for many years. *Tapiwa* is pronounced "Ta-PEE-wa." *Tongai* is pronounced "TONG-gi," rhyming with "gong guy." *Zeka* is pronounced "ZAY-ka," rhyming with "make a." For best effect, place NARRATOR 1 at far left, and NARRATOR 2 at far right, as seen from the audience.

NARRATOR 1: When Tapiwa came home from school, the police car was already in front of her house. She knew why it was there.

NARRATOR 2: Father, Mother, and her older brother, Tongai, were outside. She saw the man in the back seat rap on the window. Then he rattled the door handle so hard, it almost came off. Father went over quickly and opened it.

NARRATOR 1: Uncle Zeka stepped out. He was older than Father, and much thinner. Father was dressed in a business suit, because he had just come home from the bank. Uncle Zeka was dressed in baggy pants that had been mended so many times, they looked like a road map. His shirt was a grain bag, with holes cut out for his head and arms.

NARRATOR 2: Uncle Zeka looked at his new family and smiled. It was such a big, welcoming smile that Tapiwa knew she was going to like him.

NARRATOR 1: Father said politely,

FATHER: Have you eaten, my brother?

UNCLE ZEKA: Yes, thank you.

NARRATOR 2: . . . said Uncle Zeka, just as politely.

UNCLE ZEKA: But it is always nice to have more.

NARRATOR 1: Then Father thanked the policemen, and the family went inside. Tapiwa and Tongai sat quietly, as Mother placed dish after dish of food on the table.

NARRATOR 2: Uncle Zeka explained between mouthfuls how he had left his village in Mozambique and traveled to Zimbabwe.

UNCLE ZEKA: The bandits came in the middle of the night. They had guns, and they forced everyone outside. They took everything valuable, and when they were finished, they set fire to the huts.

MOTHER: How terrible!

FATHER: You were lucky they didn't shoot you.

UNCLE ZEKA: Some people were not lucky. After the bandits left, I searched the ashes of my hut, but there was nothing useful. I decided the only thing I could do was to come to you.

FATHER: Of course.

UNCLE ZEKA: I walked until I crossed the border. Then I walked some more, until the police found me. After that, I got to travel in a car, all the way to Harare.

NARRATOR 1: Uncle Zeka was excited about the car, because it was the first one he had ever been in. He described how the wind had blown in his face, and how things had moved past the window. He had had to close his eyes every time they turned a corner.

NARRATOR 2: From the way Uncle Zeka talked, it sounded like nothing much had happened before the car ride. But Tapiwa knew he had walked through the bush for two weeks. Every day, he had had to hunt for water and food, without so much as a pocket knife. There were lions, leopards, elephants, and hippopotamuses in the bush, as well as many kinds of poisonous snakes.

UNCLE ZEKA: Do you have a car?

FATHER: It's very old. The air conditioning doesn't work.

UNCLE ZEKA: *(sighs)* This is a wonderful place.

* * *

NARRATOR 1: For the next few days, Tapiwa and Tongai followed their uncle around. They knew it wasn't polite to talk to an adult unless he spoke to them first, but Uncle Zeka liked to talk all the time. Tapiwa asked,

TAPIWA: What did you eat in Mozambique?

UNCLE ZEKA: The same things you eat in Zimbabwe. Pumpkins, maize, fish, and caterpillars.

TAPIWA: *(shocked)* Caterpillars?

NARRATOR 2: Tongai hissed at her,

TONGAI: Be quiet!

NARRATOR 1: Later, when they were alone, Tongai said,

TONGAI: We mustn't make him feel different!

TAPIWA: I *know* people eat caterpillars. I've just never seen anyone *do* it!

TONGAI: Well, be careful. Father says it's going to be hard for Uncle Zeka to get used to things. He doesn't know how to use a telephone or change a light bulb. He can't read or write. He's just as smart as Father, but he never went to school.

NARRATOR 2: Most of the time, Tapiwa decided, Uncle Zeka wasn't any different from other village people who moved to the big city. He planted a vegetable garden in the back yard, and built a cage for chickens. Father bought him new clothes, and sandals because his feet were too knobbly for shoes.

NARRATOR 1: One night, when the air was still and thunder rumbled in the distance, Uncle Zeka invited Tapiwa to hunt termites with him.

NARRATOR 2: Here and there, termites were boiling out of the ground. Most of them were small and wingless, but among them were sleek, fat insects with wings.

NARRATOR 1: The fat insects were supposed to fly away and start new nests, but they didn't want to. The little termites ran around and bit them to make them go. Soon the air was full of clumsy, fluttering bodies from hundreds of nests.

UNCLE ZEKA: They like light.

NARRATOR 2: . . . explained Uncle Zeka, heading for a street lamp. Thousands of termites gathered there, and he and Tapiwa scooped them into a large plastic bag. Now and then, they ate one. The termites tasted slightly sour and nutty.

NARRATOR 1: All around, frogs, toads, and lizards gathered to eat. Some of the toads were so full of food, they couldn't hop.

NARRATOR 2: Under other lights, other people stood and caught termites, but Tapiwa didn't see anyone else with a large bag.

NARRATOR 1: Back at home, Uncle Zeka rolled three rocks together in the front yard and started a fire between them. He hammered out a large tin can into a flat sheet. Then he roasted and dried the termites so they would keep.

NARRATOR 2: Later, Mother cried,

MOTHER: He ruined my flower bed! There's a burned place, right in the middle!

FATHER: He didn't know it was special. He's never raised flowers.

NARRATOR 1: A few days later, Mother found a pot cooking on the kitchen stove. It smelled terrible.

NARRATOR 2: She took off the lid to see what it was.

MOTHER: *(screams)*

NARRATOR 1: Inside were dozens of fat, hairy caterpillars, bobbing up and down in a kind of soup.

NARRATOR 2: Mother took a deep breath and put the lid back on. She said to Tapiwa,

MOTHER: We mustn't criticize Uncle Zeka. The people where he lived were so poor, they didn't even have chickens. They had to eat whatever they could find. I wish, though, that he would simply eat what I cook, and not try to help out!

NARRATOR 1: That night, Uncle Zeka served his caterpillar stew. But no one wanted it.

FATHER: I'm sorry. We're not used to this kind of food.

UNCLE ZEKA: You're missing a good thing!

NARRATOR 2: . . . said Uncle Zeka, helping himself to a large bowlful.

NARRATOR 1: In the night, Uncle Zeka got very sick. Father had to take him to the emergency room at the hospital.

NARRATOR 2: The next day, he stayed in bed, looking gray and weak. When Tapiwa brought him tea, he said,

UNCLE ZEKA: I can't understand it. They looked like the caterpillars I used to eat in Mozambique. Of course, those lived on pumpkin leaves, and these were on the death-apple tree.

TAPIWA: Oh, Uncle Zeka! They were full of poison! You might have died! Why don't you just eat what Mother cooks?

UNCLE ZEKA: I want to help out!

* * *

NARRATOR 1: A few days later, Uncle Zeka announced that he wanted to hunt mice. He had an especially nice recipe for them. He took Tongai and Tapiwa to an empty lot between two houses.

UNCLE ZEKA: Mice like tall grass. There are probably *hundreds* in there, fat as pigs, waiting for us to come and get them.

TONGAI: Are we going to set traps?

UNCLE ZEKA: Traps?! We don't want just one or two! We're going to feed the whole family! Your father might even want to invite his boss.

TONGAI: I don't think Father's boss likes mice.

UNCLE ZEKA: *Everybody* likes them! Now, the best way to collect a lot of mice is to set fire to the field.

TAPIWA: We can't do that!

TONGAI: We're too close to houses!

UNCLE ZEKA: Nonsense! Grass burns so fast, it will be out before you know it.

NARRATOR 2: He gave Tapiwa a large stick, and Tongai another.

UNCLE ZEKA: Tapiwa, you stand here. Tongai, you stand over there.

TAPIWA: What are we supposed to do?

UNCLE ZEKA: I'll start the fire at the other end. When the mice run out, you hit them.

TAPIWA: I don't want to do that! I don't like to kill things!

TONGAI: Please stop!

NARRATOR 1: But Uncle Zeka was already at the opposite end of the field. He struck matches and walked along, setting a blaze.

NARRATOR 2: The fire shot up with a fierce, crackling sound. The flames were red, and the wind drove them toward Tapiwa and Tongai. Black smoke poured into the air.

NARRATOR 1: Above the sound of the fire came the squeaks of the mice. They poured out of the grass and ran straight for the children.

NARRATOR 2: Tongai stood hypnotized, and Tapiwa dropped her stick. The mice ran between their feet and around their legs. Then they disappeared into the gardens all around.

NARRATOR 1: A fire engine clanged its bell as it came around a corner. Men jumped off and began to beat out the fire with heavy sheets of rubber. Others ran to find water.

UNCLE ZEKA: *(returning, with disappointment)* You didn't *catch* anything.

TONGAI: We've got to go!

NARRATOR 2: Tongai pulled at his uncle's sleeve, but it was already too late.

NARRATOR 1: The owners of the houses came out and grabbed Uncle Zeka. They pulled him one way and another, and shouted at him.

NARRATOR 2: Tongai ran for help.

TAPIWA: Uncle Zeka! Uncle Zeka!

* * *

NARRATOR 1: That night at dinner, Father said,

FATHER: You can't set fires in the city.

UNCLE ZEKA: I was only trying to help out.

FATHER: I know. Your problem is, you don't like to sit idle all day. We'll have to find you a job.

UNCLE ZEKA: That's an excellent idea! I know just what I can do!

FATHER: What's that?

UNCLE ZEKA: Why, I can be a cook!

ALL (except UNCLE ZEKA): *(gasp)*

The Kid From the Commercial

By Stephen Manes

Adapted for reader's theater by Aaron Shepard, from Stephen Manes's book
It's New! It's Improved! It's Terrible!, Bantam, New York, 1989

> For more reader's theater, visit Aaron Shepard's RT Page at
> **www.aaronshep.com/rt**

PREVIEW: Through Arnold's broken TV screen comes a boy from a very different world.

GENRE: Humor   READERS: 5
CULTURE: American   READER AGES: 9–13
THEME: Commercialism; media manipulation   LENGTH: 5 minutes

ROLES: Narrators 1 & 2, Arnold, Will, Mr. Schlemp

NOTES: Stephen Manes's *It's New! It's Improved! It's Terrible!* is a biting look at how TV tries to turn young people into mindless consumers. For best effect, place NARRATOR 1 at far left, and NARRATOR 2 at far right, as seen from the audience.

WILL: *(smiling wide, gesturing toward ARNOLD with a pointed finger, and speaking in a TV announcer's voice)* Hey! Don't change that channel!

NARRATOR 1: Arnold was almost afraid to look, but he forced himself to turn around. All the slime that had poured out of the broken TV set was gone. It had magically changed into a boy!

NARRATOR 2: The boy was Arnold's age. He was tall and skinny and blond, and had bright blue eyes and a big smile. He was wearing a Helicopter Jones T-shirt and Helicopter Jones jeans and—of course—Helicopter Shoes.

WILL: *(spins around once and dances)*

> *Helicopter,*
> *Helicopter,*
> *Helicopter* Shoes.

> We're talk-ing
> *Helicopter,*
> *Helicopter,*
> *Helicopter* Shoes.

> *(spins around again and flashes smile)*

ARNOLD: You're from the commercial!

WILL: *(smiles wider)* Not just *one* commercial! Not just *two* commercials! Not merely *three!* Hey, I'm in *twenty different commercials,* each one more wonderful than the next! Isn't that *amazing?*

NARRATOR 1: Arnold was too flabbergasted to say anything.

WILL: *(holds out his hand)* You're my special friend.

NARRATOR 2: Arnold suddenly remembered—this kid had said those exact same words in last year's commercials for those ugly prune-faced dolls.

ARNOLD: *(distrustfully)* I don't even *know* you. How'd you *get* here? Where'd you *come* from?

WILL: *(does a tap step and spins around)*

> I come from here,
> I come from there,
> But I can come
> From *any*where!

> *(in a low voice)* Costumes sold separately.

NARRATOR 2: Arnold recognized that, too. It was the commercial for Mr. Mysterio, the amazing spy action-figure.

ARNOLD: Who *are* you?!

WILL: *(bows, still smiling)* Will Flack, at your service. Now, just tell me one thing. What exactly are we selling?

ARNOLD: *Selling?* I'm not selling *anything.* Unless maybe you're interested in a broken pair of Helicopter Shoes!

WILL: Broken? What?

NARRATOR 1: Arnold picked up his tongueless Helicopter Shoe and handed it to Will.

ARNOLD: Broken. Messed-up. Ruined.

WILL: *(brightens)* Of course! This is our never-before-offered *detachable-tongue* model! It's new! It's improved! It's—

ARNOLD: Terrible!

WILL: Terrible?

ARNOLD: Terrible.

WILL: Terrible? *That's* not terrible! Terrible is . . . *(dramatically)* Worgo, the Terrible Monstrosaur. He crushes! KRRRRRASH! He crumbles! KRRRRRRAK! He chomps! MMMMMMMUNCH! *(in his regular voice)* He's *new* from ToySel! *(in a low voice)* Batteries sold separately.

ARNOLD: *(softly)* Shhh, not so loud!

WILL: HE'S SO AMAZING, I WANT TO SHOUT IT FROM THE ROOFTOPS!

MR. SCHLEMP: *(calling)* Arnold, we've told you a thousand times!

NARRATOR 2: . . . shouted Mr. Schlemp from upstairs.

MR. SCHLEMP: *Turn down that TV set!*

ARNOLD: *(to WILL)* Shhh!

MR. SCHLEMP: Arnold, did you *hear* me?

ARNOLD: *(calling back)* Sorry! I turned it down already!

MR. SCHLEMP: *(sarcastically)* *Thank* you! Good *night.*

WILL: Grouchy? *Now* there's a cure for your blues! Just—

ARNOLD: Would you stop imitating commercials for one second?! I want to know how you *got* here!

WILL: Don't be silly. *You* know why I'm here. I'm going to be in your commercial!

ARNOLD: My *commercial? What* commercial?

WILL: Stop kidding. *You* know what commercial. Any minute now we'll jump right into action. Now, what am I supposed to do? What are we selling?

ARNOLD: We're not selling *anything.* I *live* here.

WILL: *Sure* you do. At least while this *commercial's* on. *(looks around)* I know! *TV* sets! That *broken* one over there will magically turn brand-new!

ARNOLD: I wish.

WILL: No problem! All I need is the script. Or I can just make something up. Let's see . . . . "It's magic! Make your *old* TV set just like *new* with—" What are we selling, again?

ARNOLD: I *told* you. We're not selling *anything.*

WILL: Right! A *public service* announcement! "Lend a hand! Donate your used TV to the charity of your choice! Just phone the number on your screen."

ARNOLD: There *is* no number. There *is* no screen.

WILL: You can't fool *me.* I eat Brain Berries, the cereal that gives you the smarts!

ARNOLD: *(exasperated)* I keep *telling* you. This isn't a commercial! My TV just broke! And somehow you came through it from the inside!

WILL: *(still smiling, but suddenly worried) Wait* a minute. Your T-shirt! It doesn't *say* anything on it.

ARNOLD: So what?

WILL: It has to *say* something. Or at least have some little character on the front. It *has* to. It's a sacred rule!

ARNOLD: Maybe in *commercials.* But I keep telling you, this isn't a commercial! This is *real life.*

WILL: "Real life"? I don't know what you're *talking* about. But whatever it is, it's easy to fix. You need . . . . Now, just let me think. You need . . . .

ARNOLD: I'll *tell* you what I need! I need fast, *fast,* FAST RELIEF. But somehow—

NARRATOR 1: Arnold looked again at the shattered TV, then back at the weird kid who had come out of it.

ARNOLD: I don't think I'm going to get it.

The Fools of Chelm

Told by Steve Sanfield

Adapted for reader's theater by Aaron Shepard, from Steve Sanfield's book *The Feather Merchants, and Other Tales of the Fools of Chelm,* Orchard, New York, 1991

For more reader's theater, visit Aaron Shepard's RT Page at
www.aaronshep.com/rt

PREVIEW: Where but in the town of Chelm could you find thinking that is so . . . creative?

GENRE: Folktales, noodlehead stories   READERS: 8 or 9
CULTURE: Jewish (eastern European)   READER AGES: 9–15
THEME: Logical pitfalls   LENGTH: 10 minutes

ROLES: Narrators 1–4, Chelmites 1–4, Oyzar (male)

NOTES: Though Chelm is a real town in Poland, it is also the mythical home of an illustrious Jewish community of fools. "Noodlehead stories" such as these can be heard around the world, sometimes told about towns like Chelm or Britain's Gotham, and sometimes about individuals like Holland's Tyl Eulenspiegel or the Middle East's Mulla Nasrudin. For best effect, place NARRATORS 1 and 2 at far left, and 3 and 4 at far right, as seen from the audience. OYZAR can double as CHELMITE 4. The *ch* in *Chelm* isn't an English *ch,* but like gargling or hawking—a *k* with the tongue not quite touching the roof of the mouth. If you can't make this sound, you can just say "Helm" or "Kelm." *Shul* rhymes with "pull." *Mikva* is pronounced "MIK-va."

NARRATOR 1: The town of Chelm in eastern Europe is a very special place. And Chelm is special because its *people* are special.

NARRATOR 4: They are like no others—for, you see, each and every Chelmite is a sage. They are all wise men and women.

NARRATOR 2: At least, that's what they call *themselves.* The *rest* of the world considers them fools and simpletons.

NARRATOR 3: But this does not bother the Chelmites in the least. *They* know they are the wisest people on earth, and in the end, isn't that all that matters?

NARRATOR 1: Now, the sages of Chelm enjoy nothing more than to match their wits against a good puzzle or problem.

NARRATOR 4: They thrive on the challenge of solving the most complex and knotty conundrums.

NARRATOR 2: It has been that way from the beginning—ever since they built their *shul,* or synagogue.

NARRATOR 3: The synagogue, of course, serves not only as the House of Prayer and the House of Study, but also as a town meeting place. So, naturally, it was the first structure to be built in Chelm.

NARRATOR 1: The people of Chelm were digging the shul's foundation, when a disturbing thought occurred to them.

CHELMITE 3: Wait a minute. Hold everything. What are we going to do with all this dirt we're digging up? We can't just leave it here, where we're going to have our shul!

CHELMITE 1: We never thought of that!

CHELMITE 2: What indeed are we to do with all this dirt?

NARRATOR 4: Many suggestions were made, but all were quickly rejected as unworkable.

CHELMITE 3: Wait! I have it! All we have to do is dig a deep pit. And that's where we'll shovel the dirt we're digging up for the foundation!

CHELMITE 2: Hooray!

CHELMITE 1: A genius!

NARRATOR 2: The men began to dig another pit.

CHELMITE 1: Hold it, hold it, hold it. This doesn't solve anything! What are we going to do with the dirt from *this* hole?

CHELMITE 2: Well, it's really very simple, isn't it? We'll just dig one more pit! We'll make it twice as large as this one. And that's where we'll shovel all the dirt from this hole *and* all the dirt from the foundation.

NARRATOR 3: There was no arguing with this early example of Chelmic logic, and the men returned to their work.

* * *

NARRATOR 1: No one today can be certain how many pits were dug during the building of the shul, but it is certain the shul *was* built, for the *second* public building in Chelm was the *mikva,* the ritual bathhouse.

NARRATOR 4: The Chelmites decided that the mikva should come next so that, prior to each Sabbath, holiday, or special occasion, everyone would be able to bathe correctly.

NARRATOR 2: So the sages climbed the mountains and felled some of the larger trees and rolled them down the hill.

NARRATOR 3: But when the trees were at the bottom, Dovid the Barrelmaker pointed out another problem.

CHELMITE 1: Before we carry these logs into the town, we must decide which end should be carried in first.

CHELMITE 3: What do you mean, which end?

CHELMITE 2: What difference does it make?

CHELMITE 1: What *difference*? It makes all the difference in the world! Correct me if I am mistaken, but I believe each of these logs has two ends!

CHELMITE 2: Who can argue?

CHELMITE 3: Everyone can see that each log indeed has two ends. So what?

CHELMITE 1: So it is well known that the one who goes first is the one most honored! And since we have already honored these logs by choosing them above all others to use in our mikva, we must now decide which end should be *further* honored by being carried into town first!

CHELMITE 3: That's true!

CHELMITE 2: It's a good thing we thought of it!

NARRATOR 1: Now a discussion began about which end should be so honored.

NARRATOR 4: Those who were right-handed naturally thought it should be the *right* end.

NARRATOR 2: And just as naturally, those who were *left*-handed thought it should be the *left* end.

NARRATOR 3: The debate continued through the afternoon. At last, hoping the matter might be resolved by a wisdom more penetrating than their own, they presented their problem to Oyzar the Scholar.

OYZAR: If only all problems were as simple as this, how pleasant life would be. All you need to do is cut off the left end of the log. Then you will have only *one* end, the *right* end, and that being the only end *left*, it will be the *right* end to carry into town *first. (leaves)*

CHELMITE 2: Brilliant!

CHELMITE 1: Remarkable!

CHELMITE 3: You can always count on a scholar!

NARRATOR 1: So Dovid brought out a saw and cut through the wood.

NARRATOR 4: A thin round fell to the ground.

CHELMITE 3: Hooray!

CHELMITE 2: Hooray, what? The log still has two ends!

CHELMITE 1: How can that be?

CHELMITE 2: Perhaps you haven't cut off enough!

NARRATOR 2: So Dovid began again.

NARRATOR 3: His saw slid back and forth until another round fell from the log.

CHELMITE 3: Hooray!

CHELMITE 2: Enough hoorays, already! There are still two ends!

NARRATOR 1: It is written that, where we truly wish to go, there our feet will carry us. Dovid was not to be put off so easily. With fierce determination, he cut round after round, until he was too weary even to lift his saw.

NARRATOR 4: Someone else took over, also cutting round after round. But no matter how many ends were cut off, two ends still remained—even though they were at last separated by less than a foot of wood.

NARRATOR 2: Foot-long logs would never do for a bathhouse. So off they went again for Oyzar the Scholar.

NARRATOR 3: When Oyzar saw for himself the tiny stub of a log, he announced,

OYZAR: There is no need to cut any more. All you have to do is carry these logs *sideways* into town. That way, both ends will be first, and both will be honored equally. *(leaves)*

CHELMITE 2: What a brain!

CHELMITE 3: What wisdom!

CHELMITE 1: That's using your noodle!

CHELMITE 2: Let's start with this long one.

CHELMITE 3: But wait!

CHELMITE 1: What now?!

CHELMITE 3: Just look at the road. It's lined with houses! These logs are too *long* to go in sideways.

CHELMITE 2: So, what's the problem? We'll simply *tear down the houses.*

NARRATOR 1: And they did.

NARRATOR 4: Of course, the houses would have to be rebuilt.

NARRATOR 2: But that would come later.

NARRATOR 3: After all, even angels can't sing two songs at once!

* * *

NARRATOR 1: As you might expect from such lovers of puzzles, the people of Chelm spent much time inventing and answering riddles.

NARRATOR 4: Oyzar the Scholar was a riddler of some note—though usually no one could make sense of his riddles until after they were explained.

NARRATOR 2: An example: "Why does the dog wag its tail?"

OYZAR: Because the dog is stronger than the tail! Otherwise, the *tail* would wag the *dog.*

NARRATOR 3: Another: "Why does the hair on a man's head turn gray before the hair in his beard?"

OYZAR: Because the hair on his head is at least twenty years older than the hair in his beard!

NARRATOR 1: Oyzar's own favorite was more complicated.

OYZAR: What is green and whistles and hangs on the wall?

CHELMITE 2: We give up. What is green and whistles and hangs on the wall?

OYZAR: *(chuckles)* Why, a herring!

CHELMITE 1: A *herring?* A *herring* isn't green!

OYZAR: You could *paint* it green.

CHELMITE 3: But a herring doesn't hang on the *wall.*

OYZAR: If you *wanted* to, you could hang it.

CHELMITE 2: But . . . but there's never been a herring that whistled, and there never *will* be.

OYZAR: Ha, *ha!* I just threw *that* in to make it *hard.*

* * *

NARRATOR 1: By now it should be clear that everyone in Chelm was steeped in the ways of wisdom.

NARRATOR 4: Yet, as wise as the Chelmites were, there were two questions they were never able to agree upon and that remain unsettled to this day.

NARRATOR 2: The first concerns how human beings grow. Do they grow from the head *up*?

NARRATOR 3: Or do they grow from the feet *down*?

CHELMITE 3: How can you argue? When we are young, we are given our first pair of long pants, or our first long skirt. Always, these are so long, they drag on the ground.

CHELMITE 4: But as we grow, the pants or skirt keep rising until the bottoms are well above our ankles. That proves beyond a doubt that a human being grows from the feet *down.*

CHELMITE 2: No, no! It's the other way around! Just look at a line of marching soldiers. At the bottom, their feet are all on the same level.

CHELMITE 1: But when you look at their *heads,* you'll see that some are higher than others, some lower. And that shows that we grow from the head *up.*

NARRATOR 1: The other unsolved question had to do with a simple piece of bread and butter. As long as anyone could remember, it had been an accepted truth that if you drop a slice of buttered bread, it would always fall buttered side down.

NARRATOR 4: Then some of the younger sages of Chelm decided to look into the matter. When they announced their conclusion, it created an uproar.

CHELMITE 1: It's NOT TRUE that a piece of buttered bread always falls buttered side down.

CHELMITE 4: Nonsense!

CHELMITE 3: An outrage!

CHELMITE 2: To prove it, we will conduct a public scientific experiment.

NARRATOR 2: On the announced day, the town square was filled with seekers of truth. They came from miles around.

NARRATOR 3: One of the young sages held the bread, while another slowly and carefully buttered it. Then the first sage lifted the bread, with the buttered side facing the sky.

NARRATOR 1: The crowd was hushed.

NARRATOR 4: The butter began to melt.

NARRATOR 2: The sage dropped the bread.

NARRATOR 3: It fell—buttered side down.

CHELMITE 3: *Aha!* Buttered side down!

CHELMITE 4: That proves we were right all along!

CHELMITE 2: Not at all!

CHELMITE 1: It only proves that *we* buttered the *wrong side.*

* * *

NARRATOR 1: Now that you know how the people of Chelm think, and what makes them so wise, we leave *you* to answer those two unsettled questions for yourself.

NARRATOR 4: Of course, some of you might be thinking, "Why answer such questions? *I'm* no fool."

NARRATOR 2: But remember what the good folk of Chelm always say. "If you claim you are not a fool, you only show your ignorance. For is it not written that the world was delivered into the hands of fools?"

NARRATOR 3: And we ask you, is this not the world?

* * *

Mr. Twit's Revenge

By Roald Dahl

Adapted for reader's theater by Aaron Shepard, from Roald Dahl's book
The Twits, Knopf, New York, 1981

For more reader's theater, visit Aaron Shepard's RT Page at
www.aaronshep.com/rt

PREVIEW: To get back at Mrs. Twit, Mr. Twit plays his nastiest trick ever.

GENRE: Humor   READERS: 6
CULTURE: British   READER AGES: 9–15
THEME: Revenge   LENGTH: 8 minutes

ROLES: Narrators 1–4, Mr. Twit, Mrs. Twit

NOTES: Roald Dahl, author of *Charlie and the Chocolate Factory* and other kids' favorites, here gives us two of his most nasty characters. For best effect, place NARRATORS 1 and 2 at far left, and 3 and 4 at far right, as seen from the audience. Then place MR. TWIT closest to NARRATORS 1 and 2, and MRS. TWIT closest to NARRATORS 3 and 4.

NARRATOR 1: Mr. Twit was a horrid old man.

NARRATOR 4: *Mrs.* Twit was no *better.* One morning, when Mr. Twit wasn't looking, she took out her glass eye and dropped it into Mr. Twit's beer.

NARRATOR 1: Mr. Twit sat slowly drinking the beer. He was trying to think up a really nasty trick he could play on his wife.

MRS. TWIT: You're plotting something!

NARRATOR 4: . . . said Mrs. Twit, keeping her back turned so he wouldn't see she had taken out her glass eye.

MRS. TWIT: You'd better be careful, because I'm watching you like a wombat!

MR. TWIT: Oh, shut up, you old hag!

NARRATOR 1: . . . said Mr. Twit. As he tipped down the last of the beer, he saw the glass eye staring at him.

MR. TWIT: *(gasps and jumps)*

MRS. TWIT: I *told* you I was watching you! I've got eyes *everywhere.* *(snickers)*

MR. TWIT: *(stares murderously at MRS. TWIT)*

* * *

NARRATOR 2: To pay Mrs. Twit back for the glass eye in his beer, Mr. Twit slipped a frog between her bedsheets. Then he got in his own bed and waited for the fun to begin.

NARRATOR 3: Mrs. Twit climbed into bed and put out the light.

MRS. TWIT: *(screams)* There's something in my bed!

MR. TWIT: I'll bet it's that Giant Skillywiggler I saw on the floor. I tried to kill it, but it got away. It's got teeth like screwdrivers!

MRS. TWIT: Help! Save me! It's all over my feet!

MR. TWIT: It'll bite off your toes!

NARRATOR 3: Mrs. Twit fainted.

NARRATOR 2: Mr. Twit poured a jug of cold water over her head to revive her.

NARRATOR 3: When Mrs. Twit came to, the frog had just jumped on her face.

MRS. TWIT: *(screams)* Wait . . . wait a minute. That's a *frog!*

MR. TWIT: *(snickers)*

MRS. TWIT: *(stares murderously at MR. TWIT)*

* * *

NARRATOR 4: The next day, to pay Mr. Twit back for the frog, Mrs. Twit put some worms in her husband's plate of spaghetti.

NARRATOR 1: The worms didn't show, because everything was covered with tomato sauce and sprinkled with cheese.

MR. TWIT: Hey! My spaghetti's moving!

MRS. TWIT: It's a new kind. It's called Squiggly Spaghetti. It's delicious!

NARRATOR 4: She took a mouthful from her own plate, which of course had no worms.

NARRATOR 1: Mr. Twit started eating.

MR. TWIT: It's not as good as the ordinary kind. It's too squishy.

NARRATOR 4: Mrs. Twit waited till Mr. Twit had eaten the whole plateful.

MRS. TWIT: Do you want to know why your spaghetti was squishy?

MR. TWIT: Why?

MRS. TWIT: Because it was *worms! (laughs horribly)*

MR. TWIT: *(gasps and clutches throat)*

* * *

NARRATOR 2: To pay Mrs. Twit back for the worms in the spaghetti, Mr. Twit thought up a *really* clever nasty trick. One night, when the old woman was asleep, he crept out of bed and took her walking stick downstairs to his workshed. There he stuck a tiny round piece of wood, no thicker than a penny, onto the bottom of the stick.

NARRATOR 3: This made the stick longer, but the difference was so small, the next morning Mrs. Twit didn't notice it.

NARRATOR 1: Every night after that, Mr. Twit crept downstairs and added another tiny thickness of wood to the end of the walking stick. He did it very neatly, so that the extra bits looked like part of the old stick.

NARRATOR 4: Gradually, oh so gradually, Mrs. Twit's walking stick was getting longer and longer. But it was all so slow and gradual that she didn't notice how long it was getting, even when it was halfway up to her shoulder.

NARRATOR 2: One day, Mr. Twit said to her,

MR. TWIT: That stick's too long for you.

MRS. TWIT: Why, so it is! I've had a feeling there was something wrong, but I couldn't for the life of me think what it was.

MR. TWIT: There's something *wrong,* all right.

MRS. TWIT: What could have happened? It must have suddenly grown longer!

MR. TWIT: Don't be a fool! How can a walking stick grow longer? It's made of dead wood, isn't it? Dead wood can't grow!

MRS. TWIT: Then what on earth has happened?

MR. TWIT: *(grinning evilly)* It's not the *stick,* it's *you.* It's *you* that's getting *shorter.* I've been noticing it for some time!

MRS. TWIT: That's not true!

MR. TWIT: You're *shrinking,* woman!

MRS. TWIT: It's not possible!

MR. TWIT: Oh, yes it is! You're shrinking *fast.* You're shrinking *dangerously* fast. Why, you must have shrunk at least a foot in the last few days!

MRS. TWIT: Never!

MR. TWIT: Of *course* you have! Take a look at your stick, you old goat, and *see* how much you've shrunk. You've got the *shrinks,* that's what you've got! You've got the dreaded *shrinks!*

NARRATOR 3: Mrs. Twit began to feel so trembly, she had to sit down.

NARRATOR 2: But when she did, Mr. Twit pointed and shouted,

MR. TWIT: There you have it! You're sitting in your old chair, and you've shrunk so much, your feet aren't even touching the ground!

NARRATOR 4: Mrs. Twit looked down at her feet, and sure enough, the man was right!

NARRATOR 1: You see, every night, when Mr. Twit had stuck a little bit extra onto the stick, he had done the same to the legs of Mrs. Twit's chair.

MR. TWIT: Just look at you sitting in your same old chair, and you've shrunk so much, your feet are dangling in the air!

NARRATOR 4: Mrs. Twit went white with fear.

MR. TWIT: *(pointing at her)* You've got the *shrinks!* You've got them bad! You've got the most terrible case of shrinks I've ever seen!

NARRATOR 3: Mrs. Twit grew so frightened, she began to dribble.

NARRATOR 2: But Mr. Twit, still remembering the worms in his spaghetti, didn't feel sorry for her at all.

MR. TWIT: I suppose you know what *happens* to you when you get the shrinks.

MRS. TWIT: What? What happens?

MR. TWIT: Your head *shrinks* into your neck. And your neck *shrinks* into your body. And your body *shrinks* into your legs. And your legs *shrink* into your feet. And in the end, there's nothing left but a pair of shoes and a bundle of old clothes.

MRS. TWIT: I can't bear it!

MR. TWIT: It's a terrible disease. The worst in the world!

MRS. TWIT: How long have I got? How long before I end up as a bundle of old clothes and a pair of shoes?

MR. TWIT: *(solemnly)* At the rate you're going, I'd say not more than ten or eleven days.

MRS. TWIT: But isn't there *anything* we can do?

MR. TWIT: There's only one cure for the shrinks.

MRS. TWIT: Tell me! Oh, tell me quickly!

MR. TWIT: We'll have to hurry!

MRS. TWIT: I'm ready! I'll hurry! I'll do anything you say!

MR. TWIT: *(grinning)* You won't last long if you don't!

MRS. TWIT: What is it I must do?

MR. TWIT: You've got to be *s-t-r-e-t-c-h-e-d.*

* * *

NARRATOR 1: Mr. Twit led Mrs. Twit outdoors, where he had everything ready for the great stretching.

NARRATOR 4: There were one hundred balloons and lots of string.

NARRATOR 2: There was a gas cylinder for filling the balloons.

NARRATOR 3: There was an iron ring fixed into the ground.

NARRATOR 1: He pointed to it and said,

MR. TWIT: Stand here!

NARRATOR 1: He tied Mrs. Twit's ankles to the iron ring. When that was done, he began filling the balloons with gas.

NARRATOR 4: Each balloon was on a long string, and when it was filled with gas, it pulled on its string, trying to go up and up.

NARRATOR 2: Mr. Twit tied the ends of the strings to the top half of Mrs. Twit. Some he tied around her neck, some under her arms, some to her wrists, and some even to her hair.

NARRATOR 3: Soon there were fifty colored balloons floating in the air above Mrs. Twit's head.

MR. TWIT: Can you feel them stretching you?

MRS. TWIT: I can! I can! They're stretching me like mad!

NARRATOR 1: He put on another ten balloons.

NARRATOR 4: The upward pull became very strong. Mrs. Twit was quite helpless now. With her feet tied to the ground and her arms pulled upward by the balloons, she was unable to move. She was a prisoner.

NARRATOR 2: Mr. Twit had intended to go away and leave her like that for a couple of days and nights to teach her a lesson. In fact, he was just about to leave,

NARRATOR 3: when Mrs. Twit opened her big mouth and said something foolish.

MRS. TWIT: Are you sure my feet are tied properly to the ground? If those strings around my ankles break, it's good-bye for me!

NARRATOR 1: And that's what gave Mr. Twit

NARRATOR 4: his *second*

NARRATOR 2: nasty

NARRATOR 3: idea.

Mouse Woman and the Snails

Told by Christie Harris

Adapted for reader's theater by Aaron Shepard, from Christie Harris's story "The Princess and the Snails" in her book *Mouse Woman and the Vanished Princesses,* Atheneum, New York, 1976

For more reader's theater, visit Aaron Shepard's RT Page at
www.aaronshep.com/rt

PREVIEW: When Super-Snails enslave a princess, Mouse Woman has to help set things right.

GENRE: Myths, folktales
CULTURE: Native American (Pacific
    Northwest coast, U.S. and Canada)
THEME: Kindness to animals; pride vs.
    humility

READERS: 12 or more
READER AGES: 10–13
LENGTH: 16 minutes

ROLES: Narrators 1–4, Mouse Woman, Stupendous-Scavenger (male), Magnificent-Mollusca (female), Gigantic-Gastropod (male), Gorgeous-Immensity (female), Alai-l (female), Brother, Shaman (female), (Villagers)

NOTES: Mouse Woman is a supernatural being found in many Native American tales from the Pacific Northwest coast of North America. Many of these tales are retold in several collections by Christie Harris, including *Mouse Woman and the Vanished Princesses,* which received the Book of the Year for Children medal from the Canadian Association of Children's Librarians. For best effect, place NARRATORS 1 and 2 at far left, and 3 and 4 at far right, as seen from the audience. *Alai-l* is pronounced "a-LAH-ee-EL." *Grandmother* is used as a term of respect for a female elder. All Super-Snails should speak slowly and ponderously.

NARRATOR 1: It was in the days of very long ago, when things were . . . *different.* Supernatural beings roamed the vast green wildernesses of the Northwest Coast, from Alaska to California.

NARRATOR 4: One of these was Mouse Woman, the Tiny One, who could look like a mouse or the smallest of grandmothers. Mouse Woman liked everyone and everything to be proper, so she watched the world with her big, busy mouse eyes. She especially watched the tricksters. And she watched the young people they tricked into trouble.

NARRATOR 2: A number of handsome young people had vanished mysteriously—from totem pole villages, from berry patches, and from fishing stations. Mouse Woman knew what was going on. Her big, busy mouse eyes saw everything. Her busy ears *heard* everything.

NARRATOR 3: She knew who had captured the handsome young people. She knew who now wished to capture a *princess.* And she knew who would put a stop to it all.

MOUSE WOMAN: *(to audience)* Me! *That's* who. Capture is no way to treat young people. Especially when it turns them into slaves for those insufferable Super-Snails!

* * *

NARRATOR 1: Feeding for centuries on pride and everything else in sight, the four Super-Snails had become as big as whales. They grew more and more monstrous, needing more and more slaves to gather food for their gigantic bodies.

NARRATOR 4: Like everyone else in the Place-of-Supernatural-Beings, the Super-Snails also had *human* shapes in which their spirit-selves could move around. But they had become so proud of their snail magnificence, they never *used* their human shapes—except when they needed them to trap unwary young people.

NARRATOR 2: Mouse Woman scurried into the house of the Super-Snails, the most colossal house in the Place-of-Supernatural-Beings. And there they were, as big as whales, with enormous snail shells rising above their great gray sluggishness.

NARRATOR 3:   There was Stupendous-Scavenger-and-Supreme-Snail, their chief . . . his wife, Magnificent-Mollusca . . . their son, Gigantic-Gastropod . . . and the son's wife, Gorgeous-Immensity.

MOUSE WOMAN: I've come to talk to you!

NARRATOR 1:   Four pairs of eyes opened to peer through the dimness of the colossal house. Four pairs of feelers moved this way and that.

STUPENDOUS-SCAVENGER: *(disdainfully)* Oh, it's *you.*

NARRATOR 1:   . . . said Stupendous-Scavenger-and-Supreme-Snail.

MOUSE WOMAN: I want to talk about humans!

STUPENDOUS-SCAVENGER: Humans? Why talk about beings who have never had the good sense to take the Snail as their totem?

MAGNIFICENT-MOLLUSCA: Or

NARRATOR 2:   . . . said Magnificent Mollusca,

MAGNIFICENT-MOLLUSCA: the good *taste* to use the beauty of a snail to decorate their canoes or their serving bowls.

GIGANTIC-GASTROPOD: Human beings are beneath our notice.

NARRATOR 3:   . . . said Gigantic-Gastropod.

GORGEOUS-IMMENSITY: Except as slaves.

NARRATOR 4:   . . . added Gorgeous-Immensity. Mouse Woman glared up at her. It was *she* who now wanted a *princess* to serve her.

MOUSE WOMAN: That's what I want to talk about! They shouldn't be your slaves!

MAGNIFICENT-MOLLUSCA: Nonsense! They make very *good* slaves!

MOUSE WOMAN: That's not what I mean! It's bad to snatch young people away from their families!

GIGANTIC-GASTROPOD: Oh, we don't *snatch* them. They come most willingly! You know that in our human shapes our skin is as smooth and lustrous as the pearl lining of a shell. So the young people think they are eloping with the handsomest young man or woman they have ever seen.

MOUSE WOMAN: It's bad to trap them!

STUPENDOUS-SCAVENGER: *Bad?* Because it's *human?*

MOUSE WOMAN: Human?

STUPENDOUS-SCAVENGER: Certainly! When *humans* need to eat, they trap *animals,* don't they? With their snares and pits and fishnets. So, when *we* need to eat, we trap *humans.* And *we* don't even *eat* them!

NARRATOR 2: Things were not going as Mouse Woman had planned. Her shoulders drooped under her mouseskin blanket.

MAGNIFICENT-MOLLUSCA: Also, the happiness of all snails is in our hands. And the snails grow very unhappy when humans *kick* them off the trail.

ALL SNAILS (except MAGNIFICENT-MOLLUSCA): *(in dismay)* Oh!

MAGNIFICENT-MOLLUSCA: Or, worse still, when they *step* on their beautiful, fragile little houses.

ALL SNAILS (except MAGNIFICENT-MOLLUSCA): OH!

MAGNIFICENT-MOLLUSCA: *Horrible* humans! It's our duty to *punish* them!

GIGANTIC-GASTROPOD: You will have noticed we trap only humans who have been cruel to a snail.

GORGEOUS-IMMENSITY: So we are only doing our duty to our beloved snails.

MOUSE WOMAN: I suppose it's only your duty to your beloved snails that has you scanning the countryside, just waiting for some princess to step on a little snail's house!

GIGANTIC-GASTROPOD: Of course! When a *princess* vanishes, it gets *publicity.* So there's more chance that more humans will think twice before they kick another snail off a trail—or step on it!

MOUSE WOMAN: Aren't you afraid that will do away with your supply of slaves?

GIGANTIC-GASTROPOD: Pfffffffff! We'll *never* run out of thoughtless . . . careless . . . humans!

NARRATOR 3: All four Super-Snails closed their eyes in dismissal of Mouse Woman and her ridiculous ideas.

MOUSE WOMAN: You haven't heard the last of me!

MAGNIFICENT-MOLLUSCA: No, I suppose that would be too much to hope.

* * *

NARRATOR 1: Now, the Place-of-Supernatural-Beings lay in a hidden valley, high on a mountain. Towering cliffs ringed the valley, and a great thorn hedge concealed it from view.

NARRATOR 4: The mountain on one side sloped down to the sea, and right at the mountain's foot lay a village. Carved cedar houses and totem poles, all brightly decorated, edged the small beach where canoes were drawn up.

NARRATOR 2: In the house of the village chief lived the princess Alai-l, who was beautiful as a wild rose. Nearly all the high-ranking young men along the coast and up the river had come to the chief and asked to marry the princess. But the chief and his wife did not fancy any of them. None was good enough for *their* daughter.

NARRATOR 3: Alai-l was becoming annoyed. She was longing to escape the village. She was getting so desperate, she even eyed her youngest brother's invention—a wooden eagle with moving parts, and thongs to make the parts move.

ALAI-L: *(impatiently)* Why can't you make that thing fly?

BROTHER: I can create it, but only the Great Eagle Spirit can make it fly. I am sending many prayers!

ALAI-L: Well, get busy!

NARRATOR 1: Alai-l walked on along the one street of the village and just reached its end when she saw . . . a snail. Right in her pathway.

ALAI-L: *(rudely)* I suppose *you* came to marry me, *too.*

NARRATOR 4: And she kicked the snail out of the way.

ALAI-L: I've got to get out of this village!

NARRATOR 2: Alai-l headed for the beach trail. She was not supposed to leave the village without her family around her. As a princess, she carried the royal bloodline and was precious to her entire clan. But Alai-l was past caring.

NARRATOR 3: Suddenly, she came upon a young man who had been hidden by a rock.

GIGANTIC-GASTROPOD: Alai-l, my love! Come away with me!

NARRATOR 1: He was the handsomest young man Alai-l had ever seen, with skin as smooth and lustrous as the pearl lining of a shell. He held out his hand, and she took it with strange, dreamlike pleasure. Then, as if caught in a spell, she glided away with incredible speed.

NARRATOR 4: She had escaped the village by eloping with the handsomest of young men. But . . . what was happening to her? Somehow, she had no will but *his* will. She had to go where he took her. And where *was* he taking her?

NARRATOR 2: By the time they came to the colossal house in the Place-of-Supernatural-Beings, Alai-l's dreamlike pleasure had turned to nightmare.

NARRATOR 3: This was no proper village, with a proper family waiting to welcome a daughter-in-law! She glanced in alarm at the towering cliffs that walled her in.

GIGANTIC-GASTROPOD: This is where you will serve, Slave-Princess.

ALAI-L: *Slave*-Princess?

NARRATOR 1: The young man pushed her rudely into the house. In the dim light, she could see nothing at first, but only heard a big, terrible, rumbling, churning, bubbling sound. And then she made out three monstrous shapes, lying under enormous snail shells.

NARRATOR 4: With a gasp of horror, she turned to the young man. But there in his place was another monstrous shape under another enormous snail shell. It seemed to sleep, just as the other three slept, with the big, terrible, rumbling, churning, bubbling sound coming from within.

NARRATOR 2: Shuddering with horror, Alai-l cowered back into a corner. She felt a tug at her robe, and there beside her was the tiniest of old women, watching her with big, busy mouse eyes.

ALAI-L: *(softly)* Mouse Woman!

MOUSE WOMAN: Do you know where you are, Princess?

ALAI-L: No, Grandmother!

MOUSE WOMAN: You are in the house of the Super-Snails, in the Place-of-Supernatural-Beings. They captured you because you were cruel to a snail.

NARRATOR 3: Fear and remorse filled Alai-l, as she remembered the helpless, harmless snail she had kicked out of her way.

MOUSE WOMAN: Your brothers will search for you.

ALAI-L: But how will they find the way through the thorns? And how will they find the trail down the cliffs? Grandmother . . . .

NARRATOR 3: But Mouse Woman had vanished.

* * *

NARRATOR 1: Back in Alai-l's village, the alarm spread swiftly. The princess had vanished! People searched the houses and the trails. But there was no sign of her.

NARRATOR 4: Then a shaman arrived from a distant village.

SHAMAN: I will find the princess.

NARRATOR 2: She put on her dancing apron that clattered with fringes of bird beaks. She put a crown of grizzly-bear claws over her long, straggly gray hair. She picked up her medicine rattle and her white-eagle tail feather.

NARRATOR 3: Then, as the box drums throbbed through the chief's great house, she began to circle the fire in a wild leaping dance. Her dance grew wilder and faster, wilder and faster, wilder and faster—until, suddenly, she collapsed and lay as though dead.

NARRATOR 1: She lay there a long, long time, while the people waited.

NARRATOR 4: Then at last she sat up. And her eyes were the wild-glittering eyes of one who has seen things mortals do not see.

SHAMAN: I saw the Princess as my spirit-self flew about. The Super-Snails hold her captive in the Place-of-Supernatural-Beings!

VILLAGERS: *(gasp)*

NARRATOR 2: Alai-I's four eldest brothers each set off at once to find the Place-of-Supernatural-Beings. But one by one, as the weeks went by, they returned without success. Each had been defeated at last by an enormous, impassable hedge of thorn.

BROTHER: Now *I* will go.

NARRATOR 3: . . . announced the youngest brother.

BROTHER: And I will find my sister.

NARRATOR 1: Alai-I's brother built a fire and threw in offerings to the Great Eagle Spirit—offerings of fat and eagle down, of red ochre and blue paint, and of the lime of burnt clamshells. Then off he went, carrying the parts of his wooden eagle.

NARRATOR 4: As though in answer to his prayers, he went straight to the cleverly-concealed opening in the great thorn hedge. He passed through, and below him stretched an awesome valley, walled on all sides by towering cliffs. Yet there were houses in the valley.

BROTHER: The Place-of-Supernatural-Beings!

NARRATOR 2: His keen eyes searched the houses and totem poles for Snail carvings.

BROTHER: There it is. That colossal house. That is where my sister is captive.

NARRATOR 3: As he waited for the cover of darkness and the faint light of starshine, he worked carefully on his wooden eagle, fitting the moving parts together and testing the thongs that moved them.

* * *

NARRATOR 1: Night fell on the Place-of-Supernatural-Beings. In the colossal house, the great, soft, slithery-slimy monsters had settled into sleep. Their big, terrible, rumbling, churning, bubbling sound filled the darkness.

NARRATOR 4: Exhausted by her labors, Alai-l huddled in her corner. Suddenly, she felt a tug at her robe.

ALAI-L: *(softly)* Mouse Woman!

NARRATOR 2: Another tug made her rise and follow the tiny friend-of-young-people out into the starry night.

MOUSE WOMAN: Your youngest brother is coming for you.

NARRATOR 3: Mouse Woman pointed to a spot on the top of a cliff. Alai-l caught her breath. As she watched, a mechanical eagle launched itself into the air.

ALAI-L: Oh, Great Eagle Spirit, make it fly!

NARRATOR 1: The big, jerky bird soared through the air. It was coming straight toward her! It landed close by with a splintering *thud,* and Alai-l rushed to greet her youngest brother.

ALAI-L: My dear, gifted brother! Oh, but will it ever fly *up* again?!

MOUSE WOMAN: No need! See that glisten of snail slime? That is the trail out of the valley. Hurry! Hurry!

NARRATOR 4: Alai-l and her brother were off like two deer. Their horror of what was behind them sped their feet up the glistening trail, through the hedge, and on down the mountainside.

NARRATOR 2: All night, Alai-l's brother led her swiftly along animal trails and creek beds. By morning, they were near the village. But they could hear terrible sounds behind them, as if a fire were raging through the forest.

NARRATOR 3: They raced into the village.

ALAI-L & BROTHER: *(not in unison)* The Snails are coming! The Snails are coming!

NARRATOR 1: There was a terrible sound on the mountain, the sound of rocks rolling and trees crashing. The weight of the Snails' enormous bodies had started a landslide!

BROTHER: Everyone into the canoes!

NARRATOR 4: The canoes all shot out into deep water. From there, the horrified villagers watched the avalanche of trees and rocks and giant snail bodies bury the beautiful carved houses and crest poles. Then they watched the monsters as they slid on helplessly into the sea and sank—never to rise again.

NARRATOR 2: The Super-Snails were gone, but so was the beautiful village. A wild wailing rose from the canoes.

ALAI-L: It is a punishment from the spirits.

NARRATOR 3: . . . murmured Alai-l, remembering a little snail so thoughtlessly kicked. And a dozen more villagers remembered *many* little snails.

* * *

NARRATOR 1: Darkness had come again to the colossal house in the Place-of-Supernatural-Beings. But now there was no movement of enormous feelers. There was no big, terrible, rumbling, churning, bubbling sound coming from deep inside monstrous bodies.

NARRATOR 4: Now there was only a circle of people sitting around a fire, people whose skin was as smooth and lustrous as the pearl lining of a shell. For of course, the *spirit*-selves of the Super-Snails had not died. They had returned to take up their *human* shapes, and to lament their lost immensity.

MAGNIFICENT-MOLLUSCA: *(peevishly to GORGEOUS-IMMENSITY)* You *would* have to have a *princess* to serve you.

GORGEOUS-IMMENSITY: Well, I'm sorry!

STUPENDOUS-SCAVENGER: Now, now. It's only because it *was* a princess that the tale will spread far and wide. So more people will think twice before they kick another snail out of the way.

GIGANTIC-GASTROPOD: Or step on its beautiful, fragile little house.

STUPENDOUS-SCAVENGER: I've been thinking. Now that we have to start over again with *tiny* snail bodies, perhaps I won't need to be quite so stupendous.

MAGNIFICENT-MOLLUSCA: Or I quite so magnificent.

GIGANTIC-GASTROPOD: I suppose I could be a little less gigantic.

GORGEOUS-IMMENSITY: And I suppose I could be gorgeous without being such an immensity.

ALL SNAILS: *(sigh)*

* * *

MOUSE WOMAN: *(to audience)* It's all so strangely satisfying. The bigness of the Super-Snails brought them to smallness. And the thoughtlessness of the people made them more thoughtful. Somehow, it makes everything more . . . even! *(titters)*

Westwoods

By Eleanor Farjeon

Adapted for reader's theater by Aaron Shepard, from Eleanor Farjeon's story in her book *The Little Bookroom,* Oxford University Press, 1955

For more reader's theater, visit Aaron Shepard's RT Page at
www.aaronshep.com/rt

PREVIEW: Young King John might have better luck finding a queen if he could only remember his poem.

GENRE: Fantasy
CULTURE: ——
THEME: Duty vs. dreams
READERS: 8 or more
READER AGES: 11 and up
LENGTH: 18 minutes

ROLES: Narrators 1 & 2, King John, Selina, Ministers 1–3, Princess of Eastmarshes, (King of Northmountains), (Princess of Northmountains), (King of Southlands), (Princess of Southlands), (Citizens), (Courtiers), (Hockey Players)

NOTES: Eleanor Farjeon was a much-loved British children's author of stories, plays, and poems, and a recipient of the international Hans Christian Andersen Award. For best effect, place NARRATOR 1 at far left, and NARRATOR 2 at far right, as seen from the audience. SELINA is the "saucy maid," a stock figure in British theater.

KING JOHN: *(reading his poem, and writing the last few words)*

> I know you are sweeter than grassfields in June,
> And bright as the single star watching the moon.
> I long for my grass, and I dream of my star,
> Though I haven't the faintest idea . . . who . . . you . . . are.

NARRATOR 1: As the young King of Workaday finished writing his poem, Selina the Housemaid knocked on the door.

KING JOHN: *(irritated)* What is it, Selina?

SELINA: *(steps in)* Your ministers want you.

KING JOHN: I'm busy!

SELINA: "At once!" they said.

KING JOHN: Well, go tell them—

SELINA: *I've* got my *cleaning* to do.

NARRATOR 1: The King groaned and put down his pen.

SELINA: *(looking around)* While you're seeing the ministers, I could do your room, I suppose.

KING JOHN: Yes, but don't touch the desk, *please.* I always have to *tell* you.

SELINA: *(acting put upon)* Oh, *all* right.

NARRATOR 1: The King gave her a cross look as he started for the Stateroom.

* * *

NARRATOR 2: The Kingdom of Workaday wanted a Queen, and the young King's ministers had come to tell him so.

MINISTER 1: You've come of age, Your Majesty!

MINISTER 2: It's time for you to find a wife!

MINISTER 3: And of course, she must be a princess!

KING JOHN: What princesses *are* there?

NARRATOR 2: . . . asked the young King, whose name was John, because, as the old King his father had said, the name John had always worked well, and no nonsense about it.

NARRATOR 1: They did not believe in nonsense, there in the Kingdom of Workaday, and they kept their noses so close to their jobs that they couldn't see anything beyond them. But they did their jobs thoroughly—and it was the ministers' job to see that their King married a princess, and the King's job to marry her. So John made no fuss.

NARRATOR 2: The ministers consulted their lists.

MINISTER 1: There is the Princess of Northmountains, the country to the top of Workaday on the map.

MINISTER 2: And there is the Princess of Southlands, which lies at the bottom.

MINISTER 3: And there is the Princess of Eastmarshes, which lies on the right-hand side.

KING JOHN: And what about Westwoods, that lies on the left?

NARRATOR 2: The ministers looked serious.

MINISTER 1: We do not *know* what lies in the West.

MINISTER 2: No one in living memory has gone there.

MINISTER 3: No one has passed the fence that stands between us and the country beyond!

KING JOHN: Hmm. Tomorrow I will hunt Westwoods and find out.

MINISTERS 1, 2, & 3: *(terrified) Sire,* it is *forbidden!*

KING JOHN: *(thoughtfully, to himself)* Forbidden!

NARRATOR 1: And then John remembered how in his childhood he had been warned by his parents never to go into Westwoods.

NARRATOR 2: The mothers of Workaday had *always* warned their children of the dangers that lay beyond the fence. And no Workaday children ever lost the wish to get *into* Westwoods—until they grew up and got married and had children of their own. Then they warned their *own* children of the dangers they had never seen.

KING JOHN: I will hunt Westwoods tomorrow! *(starts out)*

MINISTERS 1, 2, & 3: *(gasp)*

NARRATOR 1: He went to tell Selina to put out his things, and found her leaning on her broom over his desk, reading what he had been writing.

KING JOHN: Don't *do* that!

SELINA: *(acting put upon)* Oh, *all* right.

NARRATOR 2: She began dusting the mantelpiece. The King waited for her to say something else, but as she didn't, he had to.

KING JOHN: *(coldly)* I'm going hunting tomorrow. I want you to put out my things.

SELINA: Where are you hunting?

KING JOHN: In Westwoods.

SELINA: *(in disbelief)* Never!

KING JOHN: *(exasperated)* I wish you would understand that I mean what I say!

NARRATOR 1: Selina began to dust the desk, and a flick of her duster sent the King's writing to the floor. The King picked it up angrily, hesitated, and got rather pink.

KING JOHN: *(uncertainly)* So, you *read* this, did you?

SELINA: *(still dusting)* Um-*hm.*

KING JOHN: *(waits for her to say something more)* Well?

SELINA: *(stops and looks at him)* It's a bit of *poetry,* isn't it?

KING JOHN: *(testily)* Yes.

SELINA: I thought so. Well, I think your room's about done, now.

NARRATOR 2: And she took herself out of it. The King felt so cross with her, he crumpled his poem into a ball and threw it in the wastepaper basket.

* * *

NARRATOR 1: The morrow came, and the King rode out on his white horse for Westwoods. Presently, the tall fence came in sight, and over it he jumped.

NARRATOR 2: His first feeling was of disappointment. In front of him was a barrier of brushwood. Caught in the barrier was all sorts of broken rubbish—torn pictures and broken dolls, rusty trumpets, chipped glass marbles, and useless books without covers.

NARRATOR 1: He rode through the barricade of rubbish and found a waste of flat gray sand, flat as a plate, and like a desert in size. Flat as it was, he could not see the end of it.

NARRATOR 2: The King turned his horse, rode through the barrier, and jumped to the Workaday side of the fence. Then he rode to the palace, where his ministers hailed him with joy.

MINISTER 1: Sire, you have returned!

MINISTER 2: Thank heaven you are safe!

MINISTER 3: *(anxiously)* What did you see?

KING JOHN: Nothing and nobody! Tomorrow I will go to Northmountains and begin my wooing.

NARRATOR 1: And he went to his room.

KING JOHN: *(calling for her)* Selina! Pack my trunk!

SELINA: *(enters)* Where for?

KING JOHN: Northmountains, to see the Princess.

SELINA: You'll want your fur coat and your woolly gloves.

NARRATOR 2: And she went to see about them.

NARRATOR 1: The King thought his poem might come in useful too, but on looking in his wastepaper basket, he found that Selina had emptied it.

NARRATOR 2: This made him so cross that, when she brought him his glass of hot milk at bedtime, he wouldn't say good night.

SELINA: *(indignantly)* Hmph! *(leaves)*

* * *

NARRATOR 1: The next day, the King rode to Northmountains.

NARRATOR 2: It was more than cool there, it was freezing! Some people were in the streets, but nobody so much as glanced at him.

KING JOHN: *(to himself)* I've never seen such stiff, cold faces in my life.

NARRATOR 1: The King rushed on to the palace, which stood upon a glacier on a mountaintop.

NARRATOR 2: The Throne Room was hung in white and felt like a refrigerator. At the far end, the King of Northmountains sat on his throne, and his courtiers stood in rows, as stiff as statues. At the King's feet sat the Princess of the North, completely covered with a snowy veil.

NARRATOR 1: Nobody stirred or spoke. John plucked up his courage and slid across the icy floor to the King's throne.

KING JOHN: *(to KING OF NORTHMOUNTAINS)* I have come to woo your daughter.

NARRATOR 2: The King gave the slightest nod towards the Princess at his feet. John couldn't think how to begin. If only he could remember his poem! He did his best, kneeling before the silent figure.

KING JOHN: *(reciting loudly with no thought of the meaning)*

> You're whiter than snowflakes, you're colder than ice.
> I can't see your face, and perhaps it's not nice.
> I don't want to marry a lady of snow.
> I've come to propose, but I hope you'll say no.

NARRATOR 1: Such a complete silence followed his proposal, John began to think he must have gotten his poem wrong. He waited about five minutes, bowed, and slid backwards out of the Throne Room. When he got outside, he jumped on his horse and rode back to Workaday as fast as he could.

NARRATOR 2: His ministers were waiting impatiently.

MINISTER 1: Did all go well?

MINISTER 2: Is everything settled?

KING JOHN: *Quite* settled.

MINISTER 3: *(gleefully)* And when will the wedding take place?!

KING JOHN: Never!

NARRATOR 1: And he went to his room.

KING JOHN: *(shivering)* Selina! Light the fire!

NARRATOR 2: Selina was good with fires, and had a splendid one burning in a jiffy. While she was tidying the hearth, she asked,

SELINA: How did you like the Princess of the North?

KING JOHN: Not at all.

SELINA: Wouldn't *have* you, eh?

KING JOHN: *(glaring)* Learn to know your *place,* Selina!

SELINA: *(acting put upon)* Oh, *all* right. Anything more?

KING JOHN: Yes. Unpack my bag, and pack it up again. Tomorrow, I'm going to see the Princess of Southlands.

SELINA: You'll want your straw hat and your linen pajamas.

NARRATOR 1: And she started for the door.

KING JOHN: Uh . . . Selina . . . um . . . do you remember how that . . . uh . . . bit of poetry of mine went?

SELINA: *(huffily)* I've got too much to do to trouble myself to learn poetry!

NARRATOR 2: She went out, and the King was so cross that, when she returned with a really hot hot-water bottle for his bed, he never said so much as thank you.

SELINA: Hmph! *(leaves)*

* * *

NARRATOR 1: The next day, the young King set out for Southlands, and to begin with, he found the journey pleasant.

NARRATOR 2: But by the time he arrived, the sun burned so fiercely that the horse could scarcely move its limbs, and sweat poured down the King's forehead.

NARRATOR 1: The royal city was as silent as sleep, and nobody stirred in the streets. The King's horse dragged itself to the palace gates. It was as much as the King could do to stagger from his saddle and find his way to the Throne Room.

NARRATOR 2: There on a golden couch reclined the King of Southlands, with the Princess lolling on a mass of golden pillows at his feet. All around the room lounged the courtiers, on gilded couches piled high with cushions.

NARRATOR 1: The Princess *was* beautiful, thought John, only very, very fat. Her father was still fatter.

KING JOHN: *(to KING OF SOUTHLANDS)* I have come to woo your daughter.

NARRATOR 2: The King's smile grew a little fatter and a little drowsier. John thought he had better begin. But words and energy failed him, and he decided to recover, if he could, his lost poem. He sank on his knees before the lady.

KING JOHN:

> You're fatter than butter, you'd melt by the fire.
> You're very much fatter than I could desire.
> When I see you, my courage commences to ooze.
> I've come to propose, but I hope you'll refuse.

NARRATOR 1: The Princess yawned in his face. As nothing else happened, John made his way out, clambered onto his horse, and ambled back to Workaday.

KING JOHN: *(to himself)* I don't think that *could* have been the poem.

NARRATOR 2: The ministers were awaiting him with eagerness.

MINISTER 1: Is everything arranged?

MINISTER 2: Are you and the Princess of the South of one mind?

KING JOHN: *(lazily)* Entirely.

MINISTER 3: And when does she become your bride?!

KING JOHN: Never.

NARRATOR 1: And he went to his room.

KING JOHN: *(wiping sweat)* Selina! Bring me an iced orange squash!

NARRATOR 2: She made them very well, and soon had one ready for him. While he drank it, she asked,

SELINA: How did you get on with the Princess of the South?

KING JOHN: I didn't.

SELINA: Didn't *take* to you, eh?

KING JOHN: Mind your place, Selina!

SELINA: *(acting put upon)* Oh, *all* right. Is that all for now?

KING JOHN: No. Tomorrow I am going to see the Princess of Eastmarshes.

SELINA: You'll want your raincoat and boots.

NARRATOR 1: And she picked up his bag and started to leave with it.

KING JOHN: Wait, Selina! Where do you put what you find in my wastepaper basket?

SELINA: It goes in the dustbin.

KING JOHN: Has the dustbin been emptied this week?

SELINA: I sent for the dustman specially! It seemed *extra full* of rubbish.

NARRATOR 2: Her answer vexed the King so much that, when she came in to tell him she had everything ready in the bathroom for a nice cold shower, he just drummed on the window with his back to her, as though she weren't there.

SELINA: Hmph! *(leaves)*

* * *

NARRATOR 1: The next day, on the journey to Eastmarshes, the King was met by a harsh and noisy wind that nearly blew him from his saddle. The countryside was bleak and damp.

NARRATOR 2: The city was built of gray stone without any beauty. Everyone seemed to be rushing here and there, shouting at the tops of their voices as they stamped about their business.

NARRATOR 1: As John neared the palace, the doors flew open, and a crowd of people streamed toward him. They were led by a girl with a short skirt and flying hair, carrying two hockey sticks.

PRINCESS OF EASTMARSHES: Can you play hockey? We're one man short! Come along!

NARRATOR 2: She thrust a stick into his hand, and he found himself dragged to a great open field behind the palace. For an hour, voices yelled in his ear, hands hurled him hither and thither, and mud spattered him from head to toe.

NARRATOR 1: At last the game ended, and the girl came over to thump him on the back.

PRINCESS OF EASTMARSHES: Who *are* you?

KING JOHN: *(weakly)* I am the King of Workaday.

PRINCESS OF EASTMARSHES: Oh, indeed! And what have you come for?

KING JOHN: To woo the Princess.

PRINCESS OF EASTMARSHES: You don't say! Well, go ahead!

KING JOHN: *(stares at her)* But . . . *you* . . . aren't . . . .

PRINCESS OF EASTMARSHES: Yes, I am. Why not? Go *to* it!

NARRATOR 2: John made a wild effort to muster his thoughts and get hold of his lost poem.

KING JOHN:

> You're louder than thunder, you're harsher than salt.
> We're made as we're born, so it isn't your fault.
> My tastes are not yours, and your manners not mine.
> I've come to propose, but I hope you'll decline.

PRINCESS OF EASTMARSHES: Well, I never!

NARRATOR 1: And lifting her hockey stick over her head, she made for him.

NARRATOR 2: John scrambled to his horse and put it to the gallop. At last the young King came, muddy, weary, and breathless, to his own door.

MINISTER 1: Greetings, sire!

MINISTER 2: Are you and the Princess of the East agreed?

KING JOHN: Absolutely!

MINISTER 3: And when will she name the happy day?!

KING JOHN: NEVER!

NARRATOR 1: And he rushed to his room.

KING JOHN: *(exhausted)* Selina! Come and turn down my bed!

NARRATOR 2: Selina was very quiet and deft about it, and soon had it looking invitingly restful and ready. As she put out his dressing gown and bedroom slippers, she asked,

SELINA: What do you think of the Princess of the East?

KING JOHN: I don't!

SELINA: Hadn't any *use* for you, eh?

KING JOHN: You forget your place, Selina!

SELINA: *(acting put upon)* Oh, *all* right. Will that do, then?

KING JOHN: *(turning on SELINA)* No, it won't! *Nothing* will do till I FIND MY POEM!

SELINA: Your poem? That bit of poetry, do you mean? Well, why couldn't you say so before?

NARRATOR 1: And she took it out of her pocket.

KING JOHN: *(exasperated)* You had it all the time!

SELINA: Why *shouldn't* I? You threw it away! *(getting angry)* And a *nice* way to treat your work! A person that can't respect his work doesn't deserve to *do* any!

KING JOHN: *(backing down)* I . . . I *do* respect it, Selina. I was *sorry* I crumpled it up and threw it away. I only did . . . because *you* didn't like it.

SELINA: I never said so.

KING JOHN: *(hopefully)* Well . . . *did* you?

SELINA: It was all right.

KING JOHN: *(joyfully) Was* it, Selina? Oh, Selina, I've forgotten it! Read it to me!

SELINA: That I shan't! Perhaps it'll teach you another time to *remember* what you write, before you throw it away!

KING JOHN: Wait! I *do* remember! Listen! *(takes SELINA's hand)*

> You're nicer than honey, you're kinder than doves.
> You're the one sort of person that everyone loves.
> I can't live without you, I cannot say less.
> I've come to propose, and I hope you'll say *yes.*

SELINA: *(looks uncomfortable, says nothing)*

KING JOHN: *(anxiously)* Wasn't that it?

SELINA: More or less.

KING JOHN: *(softly)* Selina, say yes!

SELINA: Ask me in Westwoods.

KING JOHN: Westwoods?! Then do *you* go to Westwoods?

SELINA: Yes, all the time! On my days off.

* * *

NARRATOR 1: The King and Selina set off for the fence that divided Workaday from Westwoods. They followed the slats of the fence, while Selina tapped each one and counted under her breath. When they came to the seven-hundred-and-seventy-seventh slat, Selina slipped her finger through a hole and tripped a little catch. The slat swung back like a narrow door, and Selina and the King squeezed through.

NARRATOR 2: The King could hardly believe his eyes. There, as before, was the barrier of branches. But the branches were living, and full of singing birds.

NARRATOR 1: It was easy to find a way through the flowers and leaves to what lay beyond, for Selina led him by the hand. Instead of a gray stretch of desert sand, the greenest of plains stretched before them, filled with gay streams and waterfalls, and groves of flowering trees.

NARRATOR 2: Everything was bathed in radiant light, like mingled sun and moonshine.

KING JOHN: *(wonderingly, looking at everything but SELINA)* Oh, Selina! Why did our parents forbid us to come here?

SELINA: *(in a different, lovely voice)* Because they'd forgotten, and only knew that in Westwoods there is something that is dangerous to Workaday.

KING JOHN: What is it?

SELINA: Dreams!

KING JOHN: But why did I not see all this when I came before?

SELINA: Because you didn't bring anything or anyone *with* you.

KING JOHN: And this time I've brought my poem.

SELINA: *(softly)* And me.

NARRATOR 1: The King looked at Selina for the first time since they had entered Westwoods, and he saw that she was the most beautiful woman in the world.

KING JOHN: *(wonderingly)* Selina, are *you* a princess?

SELINA: I am, always—in Westwoods.

KING JOHN: *(determined)* Where is my poem, Selina?

NARRATOR 2: She gave it to him, and he read aloud,

KING JOHN:

> I know you are sweeter than grassfields in June,
> And bright as the single star watching the moon.
> I long for my grass, and I dream of my star,
> Though I haven't the faintest idea who you are.

> Oh, Selina . . . will you marry me?

SELINA: Yes—in Westwoods.

KING JOHN: *(exultantly)* And *out* of it, *too!*

NARRATOR 1: And seizing her hand, he pulled her after him, through the hedge of birds and flowers, to the other side of the fence.

KING JOHN: *Now,* Selina! Will you?

SELINA: *(in her usual voice)* Will I *what?*

KING JOHN: MARRY me, Selina!

SELINA: *(acting put upon)* Oh, *all* right. *(then gives KING JOHN her princess smile)*

NARRATOR 2: And she did.

NARRATOR 1: And on the day of the wedding, the King removed for good the seven-hundred-and-seventy-seventh slat in the fence between Workaday and Westwoods,

NARRATOR 2: so that any child—

NARRATOR 1: or *grownup*—

NARRATOR 2: could slip through,

MINISTERS 1, 2, & 3: *(happily)* forever after!

Author Online!

For more reader's theater, visit
Aaron Shepard's RT Page at

www.aaronshep.com/rt

About the Author

Aaron Shepard is the award-winning author of numerous picture books, as well as many stories in magazines like *Cricket* and Australia's *School Magazine*. Between 1986 and 1991, he was a professional actor in Chamber Readers, a non-profit reader's theater troupe performing since 1975 in the schools of Humboldt County, California. During his five years with the troupe, he scripted and directed many of its performance pieces and led workshops for teachers and students. In 1986 and 1987, he also performed, scripted, and directed for the Radio Readers, on local public radio.

Aaron left professional reader's theater in 1991, when he moved from Humboldt County to pursue his career as a children's author. But in 1993 he published *Stories on Stage* (H. W. Wilson), considered by many the premier collection of reader's theater scripts. This has been followed by the additional reader's theater books *Folktales on Stage* and *Readers on Stage,* both in 2004.

Since 1994, Aaron has shared scripts on the Internet through his acclaimed series Reader's Theater Editions. First run as an email service, the series found its current home on the Web in 1996 as part of Aaron Shepard's RT Page (www.aaronshep.com/rt). Today this is the Web's most popular reader's theater destination, with visits by thousands of teachers and librarians each week.

Aaron now lives in Olympia, Washington.

Printed in the United States
52210LVS00001B/71-152